Guide
to
Writing
for
Children

by **Jane Yolen**

Publishers   THE WRITER, INC.   *Boston*

"Cocoon," by David McCord, was originally published in *The New Yorker* Magazine in 1932; later in *Far and Few* (1952, Little Brown & Co.). Reprinted by special permission of the author.

Library of Congress Cataloging in Publication Data

Yolen, Jane.
  Guide to writing for children / by Jane Yolen.
    p.   cm.
  BIbliography: p.
  Includes index.
  ISBN 0-87116-155-9 : $12.95 (est.)
  1. Children's literature—Authorship.   I. Title.
PN147.5.Y58   1989
808.06'8—dc19   88-34577
                                              CIP

MANUFACTURED IN THE UNITED STATES OF AMERICA

CONTENTS

To all of my students, who have taught me so much . . .

And to the wonderful friends I've made in a half-life of children's books, but especially Sue Alexander, Lin Oliver, and Steve Mooser of the Society of Children's Book Writers.

*Books should be tried by a judge
and jury as though they were crimes . . .*
　　　　　　　　　　—Samuel Butler

Preface

"Books change lives," John Leonard once wrote in *The New York Times*. Although he was not talking about children's books, he should have been. No literature so transforms the reader as does the literature of childhood: shaping, molding, uplifting, explaining, and informing.

And yet in the world of books, those earmarked for children are called "juveniles," a word that carries pejorative connotations. After all, we do not call adult books "seniles." College courses in the subject are often nicknamed "Kiddy Lit," which is both cute and condescending, and are often shoved into a corner of the Education Department, away from the study of literature.

Children's book writers and illustrators are often approached by well-meaning relatives and friends who ask—with the kindest of intentions—"When are you going to grow up and write a *real* book?" meaning, of course, an adult book. Yet none of those well-intentioned folk would ever ask a pediatrician: "When are you going to grow up and look at adult throats?"

In fact, most authors of children's books agree that they do not write for a specific child (though Charles Dodgson certainly did when he took the Liddell sisters for a boat ride and told them the story that became *Alice's Adventures in Wonderland*). And many do not write specifically for children. Rather we tell stories to the child inside of us.

When I write, the audience I have in mind is the child I was, greedy for tales of adventure and magic and romance and heroism. I begin at the beginning and finish at the story's natural end, with no other goal in mind than telling that story well. Sometimes what I write is a tale for small children; sometimes for what is called the "middle-aged child"; and sometimes for that rare beastie first identified less than thirty years ago in library circles as the Young Adult. Any designation of readership is after the fact, the prerogative of the editor in consultation with the sales department. And sometimes that readership is so wide (or so unidentifiable) that the book is labeled *For All Ages*.

When I was a child hungry for books, I read everything I could get my hands on: folk tales, fantasy, poetry, Nancy Drew, Uncle Wiggly, the Mother West Wind stories, the Bobbsey Twins, and anything by T. H. White, Rudyard Kipling, James Thurber, Robert Louis Stevenson, Louisa May Alcott, Frances Hodgson Burnett, E. B. White, and Albert Terhune. I have reread many of those books since. Some of them have stood the test of the ages—my age as well as theirs. Others have been replaced by newer favorites: Natalie Babbitt, Lloyd Alexander, Patricia McKillip, Patricia MacLachlan, Richard Kennedy, Maurice Sendak, William Steig, Sid Fleischman, Patricia Wrightson, Diana Wynne Jones.

The effect of all the books I read as a child was visceral. I believe it is that way with all child readers. We take the book into ourselves, and it becomes ourselves: blood and sinew and bone.

It was with a shock of wonderful recognition that at age

25 I happened again upon one of the first books I had ever read. I hadn't thought of that book in years and probably could not have named it if threatened. Yet when I came upon it, I knew it at once.

I was sitting on the floor of my office in front of a great bookcase having just been hired as an assistant editor at Alfred A. Knopf. The editor-in-chief had suggested I go through the Knopf backlist to familiarize myself with the firm's stable of authors and artists. I had worked my way through the A's and B's and had just reached the C's when my fingers fell upon a familiar book spine. I picked it off the shelf and memories came flooding back to me. I could see vividly in my mind's eye the rug on the floor of the children's room at the Newport News, Virginia, public library where I had first read the book. It was Warren Chappell's *The Pleasant Pirate*. Perhaps it was not the world's greatest book, but it had been a particular childhood favorite of mine. The feel of the book in my hand, Chappell's carefully stylized drawings, and the story of the not-so-fierce pirate carried me to a time and place I had long since forgotten—or so I thought. Perhaps it was no mere coincidence that the first book I ever had published was *Pirates in Petticoats*.

If children react that viscerally to their books, then we who write for them must replicate that experience. Therefore, my one unbreakable rule for writing for children is this: *If you want to be a writer of books for children, be a reader of children's books*. Read all the good books you missed in your childhood. Read the ones you remember fondly from those days. Some of them will surprise you. Go to the library and cultivate the children's librarian. Browse in bookstores. Read to your own children or grandchildren—or someone else's. Volunteer to read in the local elementary school. Read the award winners and the runners-up. As you read, you will unconsciously begin to form your own opinions about what makes a good book for children.

Because writing good books for children is what this book is about. And the object of this book is threefold:

- To show you the broad view of children's book publishing. What was once a fireside tale is now big business.
- To show you the wide range of children's books. It extends from the fairy tale adaptation to the realistic novel about drugs, AIDS, divorce and death; from the rhymed picture book to the fully articulated historical novel; from the informational tome to the space opera that leaps from star to star to star.
- To show you the many opportunities open to anyone who wants to try writing for children.

However, Arthur Ransome said it plainly: "You write not for children but for yourself. And if by good fortune children enjoy what you enjoy, why then you are a writer of children's books . . . no special credit to you, but simply thumping good luck!"

—Jane Yolen
Hatfield, Massachusetts

Listen attentively, and above all remember that true tales are meant to be transmitted—to keep them to oneself is to betray them.

—Eli Wiesel, *Souls on Fire*

‖ 1

Once Upon All Times

IN SCHOOL WE ARE TAUGHT a lot of rules about writing: write about what you know; write with clarity; use proper grammatical constructions; never use the semicolon unless desperate, and then use it sparingly; don't overuse the exclamation point or the dash, but rather make the sentence itself exciting. Those are all good sensible-shoe rules. However, no one ever wrote a masterpiece attending only to such rules.

Did Natalie Babbitt have a close working knowledge of the spring of the waters of eternal life when she wrote *Tuck Everlasting*? Did Lewis Carroll fashion *Alice in Wonderland* with absolute clarity? Do Virginia Hamilton's characters speak grammatically? Did Rudyard Kipling neglect the semicolon? Did Emily Dickinson leave her dashes and exclamation points downstairs in her Amherst home?

The ordinary rules of writing are to be followed only up to

a point, and then the true storyteller must go one step beyond; more than using the well-known five senses of sight, hearing, taste, smell, and touch. Those five regular soldiers march along quite well in the army of mundane adult writing. But the sixth sense is the most important: the sense of wonder. Some people call it imagination, some genius, but I just call it wonder.

Recapitulating childhood

To biologists, those special traits and physical characteristics we have as children are called *juvenile* or *neotenic:* large eyes, the ability to learn language, curiosity. Some of us carry such neotenic characteristics into adulthood. Movie stars with large, moist, childlike eyes look vulnerable and infinitely appealing. The top linguists can learn new languages and odd grammars as easily as a child of two or three.

The best writers retain a child's curiosity, that child's sense of wonder. It pushes the writer to ask the question we all asked as children: *what if?* It is the storyteller's basic query: *what if?* What if there were dragons or deathstars, giant peaches or talking spiders? What if wishes were horses or tuning forks a way into the past? What if wolves could mother lost babies or little girls mother lost boys? What if a sleepy child fell down a rabbit hole and played croquet with a pack of cards? What if?

Of course the sense of wonder is useless without something else—the ability to be endlessly self-involved, which is another neotenic characteristic retained from childhood. After all, a writer has to spend hours without another soul around, putting down his or her thoughts onto the page. And the writer has to believe that what he/she has to say will be as fascinating to the reader. It is a monologue, not dialogue, but a monologue on which the writer hopes a good many readers will want to eavesdrop.

If you have ever watched a child at imaginative play, speaking in voices for various dolls and serving up invisible tea and cookies, you have seen an incipient storyteller at work. The mature storyteller carries into adulthood that childhood trait.

Chicken and egg

Let us suppose that you have cultivated your sense of wonder from childhood and that the words *what if* are an important part of your writer's vocabulary.

The next step is to understand where stories come from.

There are two places all stories begin: one is physical, touchable, knowable. The other lies deep in the hidden recesses of the heart.

Think of a map. It is a mere squiggle of lines on a page until at one special moment, you see the very mountains, valleys, rivers, lakes that match those squiggles. It has become real. So, too, does a story take shape.

The Japanese have a word for it: *saku-taku-no-ki.*

Saku—the special sound a mother hen makes tapping on an egg with her beak.

Taku—the sound the chick makes tapping from within.

No-ki—the moment the tappings come together.

Saku-taku-no-ki—the instant that the chick pecking on the inside and the mother pecking on the outside reach the same spot. The egg cracks open. New life emerges.

In just that way a story begins, with the physical tap-tapping on the outside. It may be a line of a song that haunts you, an article in a newspaper that piques your interest, a fragment of conversation you can't get out of your mind, a photograph or a painting that touches you deeply, a repeating dream. And then—usually later—

comes the answering emotion that tap-taps from within. Sometimes they happen simultaneously, more often they are days, weeks, months, even years apart.

My story "The Girl Who Cried Flowers" began with a Botticelli painting "Primavera." The exquisite figure of spring trips daintily across the painting, flowers spilling from her mouth. For my tale I moved the flowers to her eyes, having just completed writing a story in which words of ice cascaded from a girl's mouth. No sense repeating myself. I wrote two pages and then stopped. I had a character and a piece of magic, but no story. The tapping was on the outside, but nothing from within. The story sat in my files incomplete for five years. And then a friend who was having marital problems moved in with us. She was an artist, and her husband wanted her to paint only for him. *Saku-taku-no-ki.* "The Girl Who Cried Flowers" became the story of a girl whose young husband did not want her to be sad, so forbade her to cry flowers for the villagers ever again. In other words, he forbade her to use her one talent. My story ended magically. Story has its own logic, which real life so often lacks.

The Second Creator

Once a story is completed, it belongs to the reader, not the author. In a sense, every book is created not by a single person but recreated by everyone who reads it, literature being an unnatural act between two consenting individuals, author and reader.

Everyone who reads a story brings along his or her own psychological baggage, reading the story he or she needs to read, which is not necessarily what the author intended.

For example, the first time I read "Snow White," I identified totally with the princess. I had a real *frisson* of fear every time the wicked queen came to the cottage with the poisoned apple, the bodice strings, and the poisoned comb. Combined with the story's dangers were the dangers any child growing up in New York City faced. I had been warned again and again not to open the apartment door to strangers, but to check out callers through the peephole first. The last time I read "Snow White," I had a sixteen-year-old daughter ("Lovelier than thou, oh queen"). There was nothing I desired more than to put her in a glass casket, pipe in rock music, and let her wait there until the right college acceptance, the right job, or the right man came along. I doubt if any of those feelings were in the mind of the original long-ago storyteller who first told the tale of "Snow White" to the attentive listeners.

If each reader remakes the story in his or her image, whom should the writer write for?

Write for the child within you.

Write about those things that made you happy, angry, fearful, troubled, hopeful, curious, tender, terrified, satisfied, mollified, gratified. Reach deep inside yourself and find out who you were before you became what you are, and then you will discover that the child is there, very much alive, and informing most of your adult decisions. The person you find there is no stranger. It is your oldest, dearest friend.

The child within

We do not put away childish things when we grow up; we simply give them different names. Hopscotch players become tennis buffs, jacks enthusiasts take up knitting, skip rope champs learn ballroom dancing, stickball players watch the World Series on television, and the child who used to read under the covers with a flashlight buys a bedside reading lamp and falls asleep with her glasses perched on her nose.

So, how do you reach the child you were in order to write for children today?

I want to offer three steps, not the *only* three but three to start with, in order to put you in touch with the inner child. They are merely exercises to bring you in touch with the child you once were.

1. *Sense of wonder:* Children are born with it and too often are educated out of it. Relocate your sense of wonder. Buy a bird identification book or a wildflower book or a star map. Go outside and sit in a meadow or a park or on a boat. Just look, listen, feel, but do not talk. Adults use talk in place of feelings. Learn the name of something new every day, and try to find out *why* it is called that (windstrife, gillyflower, ovenbird, Betelgeuse).

2. *The story anew:* Can you remember the first time you read or heard Cinderella or Snow White or Jack and the Beanstalk? Find a collection of fairy stories or folktales and read one story aloud every night for a month. Or buy a storytelling tape, and listen to one story a night. Or read a story a night into a tape recorder, and listen to it the next morning while eating breakfast. I call this *The Scheherazade Method.*

3. *The outer and the inner ear:* Lullabies were our very first songs and our very first poems. Play a tape or recording of lullabies. The connotations of love and succor such songs carry will help you recall your childhood. Be sure some of the lullabies are in a foreign language, because when you were an infant, all languages were foreign to you. What you understood came through the tone of your mother's or father's voice. The la-la-las were as meaningful as the words.

Take joy

Finding the child within, writing honestly, connecting the outer and the inner tappings will all help you write the very best stories for young readers. But perhaps most importantly, you must write with joy.

The medieval monk Fra Giovanni wrote: "The gloom of the world is but a shadow; behind it, yet within our reach, is joy. Take Joy."

When I was in college writing poetry, I was plunged into adolescent cynicism and despair by the poems I wrote. My world reflected my poetry, and I lived through a mirror darkly. As I penned poems about lost love, nuclear holocaust, hypocritical religions, it was clear I saw myself as a sensitive flower holding its lovely head above such tragedies. I began to believe in the nihilistic world I invented. Yet today, writing books for children, even though I am more aware of the world's problems than when I was a teenager, I am filled with joy. The books I write, touching the child center, give me hope.

This does not mean there should be no sadness in children's books. Once upon a time does not necessarily mean happy ever after. I still remember the wonderful pain of reading and crying over Beth's death in *Little Women;* Charlotte's farewell in *Charlotte's Web;* the brave stand of the wolves and Akela's death sung in Phao's funeral oration in *The Jungle Books:* "Howl, dogs. A wolf has died tonight."

Sometimes my own stories have a darkness in them, the happy endings bittersweet and mixed with tears. In *Greyling* the selchie child returns to the sea, leaving his adopted parents on shore. Danina, in *The Girl Who Loved the Wind*, chooses to sail away from the enclosed mansion of her father's heart. In *The Pit Dragon Trilogy*, teenagers Jakkin and Akki are not able to save their beloved dragon Heart's

Blood nor solve their planet's problems. Yet behind each sadness there is hope or courage or promise or joy.

Beth's death unites her sisters. Charlotte leaves behind two legacies—her children and a much wiser Wilbur. Akela's death in battle has been noble and nobly sung. Greyling returns once a year to visit his landlocked parents and to share with them the beauties of the wide and deep sea. Danina is sailing *away from* but also *toward*—away from her overprotected youth and toward the ever-changing and ever-challenging world. Jakkin and Akki return to the dragon nursery with the hope that they can work to bring about a new and better order some day for their world.

The moral of the story

To write a story is to tap a vein. Some writers go for the jugular; others settle for lesser branches. But all writing should be approached with passion, whether it is a passion for a subject, a character, a theme, or a twist of plot. If you are not involved, you will not involve your reader, especially if that reader is a young person. As C. S. Lewis wrote in *An Experiment of Criticism*: ". . . the first reading of some literary work is often . . . an experience so momentous, that only experiences of love, religion, or bereavement can furnish a standard of comparison."

However, this does not mean that every story should point a moral; and any moral should be implied, not stated.

The earliest books for children were didactic tomes. John Foxe's *Actes and Monuments of These Latter Perilous Days*, known more familiarly as *Foxe's Book of Martyrs*, was the Puritan child's bedside companion. Young readers were instructed to emulate the religious martyrs, and much detail was spent on each maiming, torture, and dying words of those worthies. Illustrated throughout, the book had a clear message. The threat of Hell hung heavily over the young reader's head.

In the nineteenth century, moral didacticism in children's books took a different route. The new threat was the threat of Information. Each story was meant not to amuse but to instruct. Every word was weighted with teaching, freighted with facts.

Moralism and didacticism are widespread today, though they are disguised by slicker covers and smoother approaches. Fundamentalist groups lobby to remove from library shelves such books as *The Wizard of Oz* (it has good witches), *The Diary of Anne Frank* (non-Christians treated sympathetically), *Making It With Mademoiselle* (under the mistaken impression that this pattern book culled from the pages of *Mademoiselle* magazine was a sex manual). Their attacks are matched from the left by groups agitating for the removal of such books as *Huckleberry Finn* (because the slave is known as "Nigger Jim").

There are, of course, many wonderful books written by authors motivated by creative outrage, books powerfully written, with a shining honesty and a fine eye for history. Ann Turner's *Nettie's Trip South*, about a young white girl's first journey through the slave state; Jamake Highwater's *Legend Days*, concerning the treatment of Native Americans; Katherine Paterson's *The Great Gilly Hopkins*, about a terrified and difficult foster child; Julius Lester's *To Be A Slave*, a culling of powerful slave narratives presented for young readers. But in each case we are moved by the story first—and the morals afterward.

Story first. The great storyteller Isaac Bashevis Singer wrote: "Truth in art that is boring is not true." Surely we all have morals inherent in our lives. My moral sense may not be the same as yours. But the characters I create will live as my moral values dictate, because they are bone of my bone, blood of my blood. They will live if I let them have life; not by *dictating* to them, but by *listening* to them.

And so will yours.

I only write when I am inspired. Fortunately I am inspired at 9 o'clock every morning.

—William Faulkner

‖ 2

And Where Do You Get Your Ideas?

WHENEVER I SPEAK to groups of adults or children, I am asked the same question: Where do you get your ideas? As if ideas are sent in the mail or purchased from a catalogue or found along the roadside, having been discarded by some unartistic type.

And yet, in a very real way, I *have* gotten ideas in the mail, from catalogues, and along country roads. A friend sent me a letter asking me to write a dragon story for an anthology he was editing. That story, "Cockfight," became the genesis for the entire *Pit Dragon Trilogy*. Another time I bought a bird feeder from a catalogue; it lured many house finches to my kitchen window. I wrote a poem about their greedy feeding, which I've included in a poetry collection for children. Again, along the roadside I have discovered many ideas: the setting for *The Inway*

Investigators, the island and lighthouse for the story "One Old Man with Seals," the flat, Thessalian plain in which *The Boy Who Had Wings* takes place.

I have also garnered ideas from newspaper stories, photographs, paintings, rock-and-roll songs, folk songs, books, movies, overheard conversations, tombstones, shop windows, mirrors, my own children's antics, and dreams. In other words, *ideas are everywhere.* The images of sight, sound, touch, taste, and smell surround us. We ingest them without realizing it and file them away. The mind is a scrap heap.

Some scraps are immediately accessible: phone numbers of friends, the grocery list, your children's birthdays, your father's favorite shaving lotion, the words of a special song.

Other scraps have been shoved back so far, you believe them lost forever. But they are not gone. They are simply waiting there, ready for use, often popping into your head when you least expect them.

When those bits and pieces, long forgotten, suddenly float to the surface, it is called *inspiration.*

Creative memory

Ezra Jack Keats, in relating how he put together his Caldecott-winning book, *A Snowy Day*, said that he saved patterned pieces of wrapping paper that fascinated him, color pages from old *Life* magazines that caught his eye, bits of material, and wallpaper samples. And one day, these bits and pieces evolved into the bright collages for his book. In other words, he transformed the contents of his scrap basket with the glue and stickum of his imagination into the story of a small boy and his adventures in the snow.

Not quite so obviously, the writer performs this same kind of magic.

The following two examples show how my own scrap

basket mind has worked. They illustrate what creative writing teachers *really* mean when they caution, "Write about what you know." Since my books have included stories about pig butlers and princesses, seal boys and Shakers, dragons, lady pirates, and space-faring toads, I cannot have taken that advice literally. And yet I have really known all of these characters in the way that counts.

In terms of my "creative memory"—that part of me that embroiders my personal experiences and transmutes them into fancy—I know pig butlers and princesses, seal boys and Shakers very well. All the faraway places I write about are really home.

The Emperor and the Kite came from a single sentence I first saw in a year's worth of research I was doing on kites when my father, then International Kite Flying Champion, was writing *The Young Sportsman's Guide to Kite Flying*, and I was helping him. In a gigantic multi-volumed work called *Science and Civilization in China*, I came upon the sentence "The Emperor Shun was rescued by his daughter from a tower prison by means of a kite." I noted it down on a 3" × 5" card, but it was not used in my father's book.

Some five years later, the sentence pushed its way into my consciousness. I wondered how a princess could have accomplished such a thing. And before I could stop myself, I had begun a tale about a Chinese princess so small and ill-thought-of that she played all alone in the palace garden with only a kite for company.

Princess Djeow Seow did not look very much like my father (though he was a small man, an important fact of his life), but her love of kites bore a striking resemblance to his. Her desire to please her own father, which led her to rescue him when her older brothers and sisters failed, was similar to my own. What began with a snippet of sentence carefully transcribed onto an index card ended happily-ever-after when *The Emperor and the Kite* was named a Caldecott Honor Book, recognizing Ed Young's brilliant Chinese papercut illustrations of my story.

That same process of inspiration, or "scrap-basketing," went to work on a folk song I had known for many years. The song, "The Great Selchie of Sule Skerry" (Child's *English and Scottish Popular Ballads*, #113), was a ballad I had learned as a twelve-year-old. It is one of those dour, tragic, magical songs that appeal to the romantic adolescent. The song tells of a classic case of faerie mismating, the coupling of a seal-man with an "earthly nourrice" or human woman. Hardly the stuff for a young child's book.

Yet some fifteen years after I had first learned that song, my creative memory went to work on one of the verses:

> I am a man upon the land,
> I am a selchie in the sea,
> And when I'm far frae every strand,
> My dwelling is in Sule Skerry.

What if—I asked myself—a selchie, a seal-man, were adopted by a human family, a childless couple. Would they try to keep him a man upon the land? Would they let him go back into the sea?

This problem of fledging is a dual one. Parent and child see it from very different perspectives. I had a brand-new infant, my first child. And as I held her in my arms, I looked ahead to the time when she would want to leave and begin her own life. So I wrote *Greyling*, in which a fisherman brings home to his barren wife a seal pup that he has found stranded in the shallows. But when he hands it to her, wrapped in his shirt, she finds it is a human child, not a seal.

The story began with the folk song and my own turbulent emotions as a new mother. But the countryside in which I set the tale came from a camping trip I had taken the year before on the Pembroke Coast in Wales. The steep cliffs that sheer off into the churning green-blue sea were waiting in the scrapbasket of my mind. They were there when I needed to make my word collage.

Such scraps are not gone once they have been used. Unlike Ezra Jack Keats's collage material, the bits and pieces stored in the mind can be used again and again.

The selchie, for example, reappeared in my story "The White Seal Maid," which I included in my collection *The Hundredth Dove* and in a poem "The Ballad of the White Seal Maid" included in *Neptune Rising*. The Great Selchie himself became a major character in my short story "Sule Skerry," published first in *The Magazine of Fantasy and Science Fiction*, and later in *Neptune Rising*. I expect to use selchies, the cliffs of Wales, and the "earthly nourrice" again some time, though I cannot predict where or when.

Idea file

There are times, of course, when inspiration gets a bit sluggish and, like a car that needs extra choking on cold days, one's creative memory can use some help.

To this end, I feel that every writer—beginning or advanced—should keep an IDEAS file.

My memory is not great, my forgettery terrific. If I don't write down that snippet of sentence or preserve the verse, it will be gone. The Vermont tombstone that read, "It is a fearful thing to love what death can touch," became important to a book seven years after I first wrote it down. The photograph I took of the Malaysian merman in a Greenwich, England, antique store swam onto the pages of a short story over a year later. I would never have kept them fresh without my IDEAS file.

Something else to keep in the file is a title list. It is a

finger exercise that, like Czerny to the piano student, can eventually lead to Bach.

Occasionally, I will sit down at the typewriter and devote a half hour to writing down titles in a variation of the old word-association game.

This is a title list I jotted down one day in 1962:

> *The Heart Wind*
> *Gomer the Rat King*
> *The Sea Witch*
> *A. Dragon & Son*
> *Dragon or Dragoon*
> *The King with Too Many Crowns*
> *The Waxworks Mouse*
> *The Man Who Grew Flowers in His Hair*

Here's what happened with those titles from 1962 to the late 1980s:

The Heart Wind made me wonder who might the wind love or who might love the wind, and I came up with the story *The Girl Who Loved the Wind*, a book which has been in print in hardcover and paperback since 1972.

Gomer the Rat King became the villain of an early reader chapter book called *Mice on Ice* (published in 1980).

The Sea Witch tried to be a story, but never worked. I cannibalized the opening sentences, incorporating them into the opening of *Greyling* (written in 1966). The witch herself became a major figure in my fantasy novel *The Magic Three of Solatia* (published in 1974).

A. Dragon & Son is still simply a title, but *Dragon or Dragoon* was the inspiration for my short story "The King's Dragon" (published in *Spaceships & Spells* in 1987).

*Both *The King with Too Many Crowns* and *The Waxworks Mouse* never became anything, though I did start a story about a rodent who lived at Madame Tussaud's, which is still waiting patiently for a plot after twenty years.

The Man Who Grew Flowers in His Hair was superseded by the story "The Girl Who Cried Flowers."

If anyone tells me it is useless to brainstorm titles or to put snippets of sentences into my IDEAS file, I laugh. After all, that half-hour's work in 1962 has produced over twenty years' worth of inspiration.

Strings that touch the sky

As a member of a kite-flying family and an inveterate string saver, I know that enough little ends of strings can eventually make a strand that can touch the sky. It works in writing, too. We build our books with loops and loops of leftover string.

If I were a scientist, I would remind myself that matter can never be lost. If I were a gardener, I would call it the great recycle of life. If I had a religious vocation, I might call it a second coming. But I am a string saver and a kite fanatic, and I see it in terms of loops.

Simply, what you have researched and written about, you can use again and again in new and surprising ways.

I wrote *Friend*, a biography of George Fox, the founding father of the Quaker religion. Because it was successful, another publisher asked me to do a book about the Shakers, another religious group which was a bizarre and radical outgrowth of the Society of Friends.

Loop 1: *Simple Gifts* was the Shaker nonfiction book. It was partially built upon the history I had researched for *Friend*. The earlier work also prepared me for understanding the group religious mind, as well as how persecuted religious minorities behave. However, as I researched this project, I kept thinking that there were surely many stories in that history that might be written as narratives. I found dozens of interesting true tales in the journals of both believers and apostates. Creating a fictional amalgam would be a fascinating task. My daughter was just fourteen and interested in boys, and it occurred to me that to set a girl just like her in a celibate Shaker community in the nineteenth century, the heyday of the Shaker religion, could be just the spark I needed for my tale: Romeo and Juliet in a household of celibate saints.

Loop 2: *The Gift of Sarah Barker* was the novel that developed from that idea. Sarah is headstrong, passionate, self-doubting, always questioning authority. When she falls in love with Abel Church, the foundations of their life in the fictional Shaker community of New Vale are shaken. I borrowed the round barn from an actual Shaker village in Hancock, Massachusetts, and the house and outbuildings from the Sabbathday Lake Shaker community in Maine. But I borrowed Sarah Barker's looks and personality from my own adolescent daughter.

Loop 3: *Dragon's Blood*, a science fiction novel set in the 24th century, came next. It, too, had a great round barn, with a description of steam rising from stored grasses that came directly from research on that Hancock Village barn. But instead of housing cows, the barn on the planet of Austar IV houses dragons. The men and women of that farm are not celibate saints like the New Vale Shakers, but the book, like its predecessor, is, in part, a love story about adolescents. The boy Jakkin looks and acts a great deal like my middle son, who was a teenager at the time I wrote the book.

Loop 4: *The Pit Dragon Trilogy.* One book grew into three. *Dragon's Blood* was quickly followed by *Heart's Blood* and, two and a half years later, by *A Sending of*

Dragons. I have a suspicion that the saga of Jakkin and the dragons is not really over. Only time will tell.

But the loop may be played out. It has been a while since I have jiggled that particular string. However, at the back of my mind, I have been toying with the idea of a young adult novel about religious millenial communities, the kind in which members sit atop a mountain waiting for the end of the world to arrive on a specific appointed day.

So nothing is really lost when one researches a book, though it may take years before a particular idea or theme is disinterred.

Loops within loops within loops.

The best kite-fliers know that those pieces of string can make a line long enough to touch the sky.

Connecting "was" and "could be"

Thus inspiration comes from the scrap basket of your brain, the sum total of your experiences. And you can make loops within loops as you start to write.

If you are lucky, those flashes of inspiration, those connections your brain makes between the *was* and the *could be,* occur when you are comfortably seated at your desk with all your writing paraphernalia in front of you.

But what about the times you are driving fifty-five miles an hour down the highway? Or the times you are washing your hair? Or the times you are in a conference? Or taking an important phone call?

That is the time your pocket-sized notebook with its attached pen is your best friend. In that notebook you scrawl the first words of a new mystery novel that won't wait until you are safely home. I had that experience in a snowstorm, while listening on the car radio to an advertisement for a fence that was, in the announcer's best New England accent, "horse-high, hog-tight, and bull-strong."

The phrase was too good to lose, but it would have been gone forever if I hadn't scribbled it into my notebook. The words sparked something immediate, and I added a few more lines which became the first paragraphs of *The Inway Investigators*, a mystery about a boy puzzled by a strange fence that has gone up suddenly on a neighbor's property:

> What makes a good fence? Grandad used to say being "horse-high, hog-tight, and bull-strong." And Uncle Henry, my guardian, winks and says, "Good neighbors make good fences." Only when I ask him what he means by that, he just laughs and says I'll understand in a while.

If I had waited until I was back home, made myself a cup of tea, and was finally back at my typewriter, I would never have remembered the words of the commercial. But since I wrote the ad down right when I heard it, at the moment it jolted me, I needed only to pop the scribble into the IDEAS folder.

Of course, if no notebook is handy, scraps of paper, backs of envelopes, paper napkins or theater programs will do.

As a youngster, I once had dinner with my father and fantasy writer Gerald Kersh at a highly respectable New York restaurant. In the middle of the conversation, Kersh got a faraway look in his eyes, reached into his pocket for a pen, and having no notebook, started to scribble on the linen tablecloth. At dinner's end, my father picked up the check, but Kersh paid for the tablecloth, taking it home— presumably for his IDEAS file.

However, just owning a notebook or Ideas folder is not enough. Your scribbles are related to real ideas the way wheat in the field is related to bread. It will take many hours, days, weeks, months, even years of winnowing, kneading, shaping—and added ingredients—to make a proper loaf.

A long patience

You may never find a way or place to use some items, and they will remain in your IDEAS file forever. What am I to make of the snapshot of the bear in the Central Park Zoo, his head coyly placed on his paws, staring directly at the photographer? It meant something to me once, but no longer.

What did I mean by that notecard in the folder that bears the scribble, "From the Apocalypse Tapestry: the woman clothed with the sun."

Or the note that the word "sciamachy" means *boxing with shadows.*

Never mind. Next year, or the year after that, one or another of my collected tidbits will speak afresh, and a book or a poem or an article or a story will be born. It has happened enough times so that I am sure it will happen again.

Notebooks and files are the perspiration that go along with the inspiration. One of the constant problems of a fertile mind is that ideas and characters and plots crowd into it, clamoring for expression. It is the author's responsibility to pick out the one voice amongst many. After all, *all art is selection.*

The French naturalist Georges Buffon contended that genius is simply a long patience. Part of any writer's long patience could be documented from the manila folder labeled IDEAS or the notebook crammed with titles, or the bulletin board peppered with snippets of sentences and interesting quotes.

Anyone who writes down to children is simply wasting his time. You have to write up, not down.

—E.B. White

‖ 3

The Pictured World

THE PICTURE BOOK is a generic term for books that are roughly half picture, half text, yet an integrated whole. They are the most popular and most easily recognized genre in children's books. And they are the least understood by would-be authors.

Picture books have the compression of poetry, the psychological rightness of a full novel, must have illustratable situations, and fit into a 32-page format.

The three most important things to know about writing the picture book are these:

- be simple
- understand structure
- find the audience within

To start with the last, the audience for picture books is variously put at ages 3-7, 4-7, or for grades K-3 (kindergarten through third grade). Yet these are books that will most often be shared adult-to-child, and so the audience is adult as well.

How do you write for such a wide audience? Again, you write for the child within. Tap the emotions and interests you had at age 4 or 6 or 7. Did you have night fears? Did you fight with your brother? Did you miss your father? Did you own a special blanket? Did you say goodbye to a dying grandparent? Did you ever bury a pet? Did you sometimes walk under the stars with your mother? Or go owling with your father? Were you adopted or fostered or an only child until your sister came? Those are all strong themes for picture books and many of them have been used—more than once.

For example, Tomie de Paola's *Nanna Upstairs, Nanna Downstairs* is about a boy whose aging grandmother lives on the second floor of his house. Patricia MacLachlan's *Mama One, Mama Two* deals with a foster family. Charlotte Zolotow's *William's Doll* is about a boy whose male relatives think dolls are sissy things for boys to play with. Margaret Wise Brown's *The Dead Bird* details an elaborate funeral arranged by some neighborhood children for a bird. My *Owl Moon* tells of a little girl and her father who go out on a winter night to call down owls. And Maurice Sendak's now-classic *Where the Wild Things Are*, with its telling economies, deals with a naughty boy who has been sent to his room.

But not all picture books are as realistic as the ones above. Some are delightfully silly like *King Bidgood's in the Bathtub* by Don and Audrey Wood. Some are historical, such as Donald Hall's *The Ox-Cart Man*, illustrated by Barbara Cooney. Some are mystical and strangely compelling, like Nancy Willard's *A Visit to William Blake's Inn*, illustrated by Alice and Martin Provensen. Some are poetic, like Uri Shulevitz's *Dawn*. Some are parables—*The*

Story of Ferdinand by Munro Leaf, with pictures by Robert Lawson. Some are simply rollicking good tales. The world of picture books is very wide indeed.

But understanding simplicity and structure is necessary to the successful writing of any of them.

Two views

There are two views of a picture book. The first is that it is a palette with words, the second that it is a story with illustrations. People who subscribe to the first view are usually artists. Most writers subscribe to the second.

Both are correct.

This leaves the author with a difficult problem. He or she must write a story that can be easily illustrated without having the illustrations overbalance the creative work of the writer. A picture book should be a partnership between author and artist, between writer and illustrator. It is a partnership that is brokered by an editor if author/artist are not one and the same. Often the writer of a picture book does not get to meet or even speak to the illustrator of the book. The story on the page must be the articulate one.

This means the author walks a very thin line between too much and too little. And like all tightrope walkers, the writer must use skill to make it all look simple.

BE SIMPLE

Simple is the operative word in picture books.

Obviously, a picture book is not a great opus, intricately plotted, full of in-depth character detail. The text/story is minimal. There should be hardly any description. Yet the picture book must have the properties of longer works; a recognizable setting, psychologically identifiable characters, a strong thematic subtext, poetic language.

But *simple* does not mean *slight*.

The classic example of a substantial story with full-blown characters, a strongly appealing theme, and a suspenseful plot done with a minimum of words is Beatrix Potter's *Peter Rabbit*. It is a simple story: a naughty rabbit, despite his mother's explicit warnings, goes into the farmer's garden. He spends the rest of the tiny book trying to escape.

Simple? Yes. *Simple-minded?* No. It has action, suspense, drama, a cast of memorable characters (Mother, a single parent, is a strict disciplinarian; dutiful sisters Flopsy, Mopsy, and Cottontail; Mr. McGregor, the frantic farmer; the helpful sparrow, who exhorts Peter to do his best; and, of course, the ever-irrepressible Peck's Bad Boy of Bunnydom, Peter himself). The outcome of Peter's adventures is in doubt until the very end. After all, Peter's father had been made into rabbit pie by the very same farmer. Mrs. Rabbit has every right to be afraid that Peter has inherited a good deal of his father's impetuous nature and very little of her sensible cautiousness. He may end up, as his father did, between crusts.

Notice the wonderfully distinct words Beatrix Potter used. They are not simple at all: *exert, scuttered, camomile*. They become a part of the listening child's vocabulary.

A book, after all, is part of the learning experience. Children at the picture book age are picking up an average of over twenty new words a day! As J.R.R. Tolkien put it: "Their books like their clothes should allow for growth, and their books at any rate should encourage it."

A final word about this idea of *simple*. As poets know, the simplest things are often the most difficult to do. Because picture books are so short (not more than ten typed pages), each word must count—especially verbs. No sloppiness of diction, no stray adjectives or adverbs, no long-winded explanations, no extra or extraneous ideas. A picture book is basically a kind of poem: economical, compressed, suggesting rather than telling. The writing of a picture book demands the same kind of attention, passion, and focus.

An example of several versions of an opening paragraph of a picture book might be instructive to show how the author achieves that compression, that exactness of language, in a story for reading aloud. After all, picture books are meant to be read aloud. If it does not please the ear as well as the eye, it will not be a good book for young children.

The book is my storybook *Greyling*. Reading the three versions will give you an idea of how each sentence is polished, words substituted (and sometimes changed back), word order inverted, words deleted. Then everything is read aloud until it is the very best I can make it.

Version # 1

THE SEA WITCH

Once on a time when wishes were aplenty, a fisherman and his wife lived in a hut beside the sea. They had all that they could eat that came out of the sea. Their hut was covered with the finest sea mosses that kept them cool in the summer and warm in the winter. They ate at a driftwood table and filled the house with sea pansies and seaweeds. There was nothing they needed or wanted—except a child.

Comment: I loved the first phrase and the last line—good, strong statements—but there is a lot of mushiness in the center of the paragraph. Too many extraneous details. Keep it simple, I reminded myself. What words did I hate the most? *Sea pansies.* And remember, that title came from my 1962 title list. As the story progressed, there was no sea witch in the tale at all. It became a book about a selchie, a wer-seal. Stories of selchie folk abound along the northern coasts of Scotland and Ireland. I just borrowed the creature and wrote my own tale.

Version # 2

SILKY

Once on a time when wishes were aplenty, a fisherman and his wife lived in a hut *by the side of the sea not far from town.* All that they could eat came out of the sea. Their hut was covered with the finest mosses that kept them cool in the summer and warm in the winter. *Sea weeds and grasses grew in gay-colored pots by the windows and doors.* And there was nothing they needed or wanted—except a child.

Comment: The additions are in italics. They are not notable either for what they add or their poetic feel. But it shows I was disturbed by those middle lines. I got rid of *sea pansies,* but *gay-colored pots by the windows* is not any better. The problem is that I am telling more than the reader needs to know. This opening should be spare, sketching in the setting. The house is important only in that it shows the fisherman and his wife comfortably settled by the side of the sea and utilizing the natural elements. Once said, it needn't be repeated. The town can come in later. And note that the title has undergone its first change. It was related to "selchie" and was, at first, the seal-child's name until my editor suggested (rightfully) that it was not a boy's name.

Final version

GREYLING

Once on a time when wishes were aplenty, a fisherman and his wife lived by the side of the sea. All that they ate came out of the sea. Their hut was covered with the finest mosses that kept them cool in the summer and warm in the winter. And there was nothing they needed or wanted—except a child.

Comment: Compression, just enough detail, and getting from the fairy tale opening right to the heart of the problem—desiring a child—in 60 short words. It reads well out loud. And it ends with that ringing, one-syllable, all-important word *child*.

In writing this book, I was lucky. It took me only three tries to get the first paragraph right. I have been known to rework an opening as many as twenty or thirty times. But whenever I begin a picture book, I remind myself of the first verse in William Blake's famous poem:

> Tyger! Tyger! burning bright
> In the forests of the night,
> What immortal hand or eye
> Could frame thy fearful symmetry?

What could be simpler than those four lines? Yet it took Blake—a genius—*seven* revisions to make the poem that simple. Certainly the rest of us can cultivate a similar patience.

STRUCTURE

If *simple* is the first thing you must keep in mind when writing a picture book, the second is *structure*. That is because a picture book is more structurally limited than any other kind of children's book.

First there are page limits. A picture book is almost always 32 printed pages. (Occasionally it is 48, but that is the exception, not the rule.) Not all of the pages, though, are allocated to text and illustration, as we shall see.

If you make a book *dummy* for yourself, stapling together a blank book with 32 pages (counting each side of the paper as an individual page), you will begin to understand the structural limitations of a picture book. Alternatively, you can make a rough sketch on a single sheet of paper that will look like this:

	1

2	3

4	5

6	7

8	9

10	11

12	13

14	15

16	17

18	19

20	21

22	23

24	25

26	27

28	29

30	31

32	

The first four to seven pages are going to be *front matter*—that is, half title, title page, copyright page, dedication. Sometimes these pages will be elaborately illustrated. Other times they will be simply in type. Check a dozen published picture books in the library, and you will see how much they differ in their use of front matter.

Why should you be aware of these mechanics? Isn't this kind of formatting the publisher's problem—not yours?

Remember, anything that is going to affect the publishing of your book is going to affect your writing. If you know about it and understand the process, then you have given yourself a head start. If you do not understand how a picture book is put together physically, you will not write a text that flows from page to page. You will not write a story that can cover 32 illustrated book pages (minus the front matter) without strain. You are likely to get rejection letters that talk about your *slight* text.

Part of understanding what makes a picture book work is understanding the role the art plays. Illustrator Diane Goode has written that "The manuscript has always been a gentle master." The master of that master is the author.

Mental pictures

Since you will not be drawing the pictures, unless you are a professional illustrator yourself, you must try to visualize as you write so that your word pictures will be accurate and tight.

Yet while you keep pictures in your head, *never* write out copious instructions to the illustrator. One of the easiest ways to recognize an amateur author is by a manuscript filled with parenthetical advice to the artist.

For example, if you wrote the following, an editor would know immediately that you are a novice:

Once upon a time there lived a witch at the bottom of the sea. (Picture: witch in regular black witch's outfit and pointed hat, with mermaid's tail, sitting on a sunken ship's prow. Her hair is spun out by the ocean. A starfish nestles in the strands of her hair.)

The instructions to the illustrator are longer than the text itself! That is a red flag to an editor: Stop! No need to read further.

Rather than instruct the illustrator, the text itself should convey all that is within the parenthesis—if that information is important. If not, then the author must trust the artist's ability.

In other words, should your witch need a particular look, begin the story that way:

Once upon a maritime, when the world was filled with wishes the way the sea is filled with fishes, there lived a witch at the bottom of the sea. She always wore a long black dress nearly covering her scaly tail. And when she sat on a barnacled prow, deep in the sunless part of the sea, she sang up bubbles and let the waves comb out her hair so that little fish could come and settle in her curls.

Otherwise, just write "Once upon a time there lived a witch at the bottom of the sea" and trust the "gentle master" to lead the artist into inspiration. Perhaps the illustration will show the witch with a starfish buckle on her hat. Or perched on a sunken pirate chest. Or riding a seahorse. Those ideas may be as good—or better—than the ones you originally dreamed.

For example, I set my story *The Girl Who Loved the Wind* "far to the East." Artist Ed Young interpreted that to be Persia and did the illustrations as Persian miniatures. In

Piggins, a picture book mystery set in a Victorian household of animals, I wrote that the house owner, Mr. Reynard, liked to invent things. Artist Jane Dyer filled the house with the fox's inventions.

The only time parenthetical advice to the illustrator is warranted is to provide information that simply cannot be conveyed by the text. Perhaps for the sake of humor, you want pictures and text to say exactly opposite things:

> It was one of Thomas's *good* days. (Illustration: Thomas is sitting under a pile of toys, roller skates on his feet, having just slid into the pile.)

In your mind's eye, you may have pictured Thomas as a little boy, but the illustrator sees him as a mouse. The editor may suggest that since there are already two upcoming mouse stories on the publisher's list, the artist try a different animal, and thus a skunk boy or an alligator child is the result.

To sum up: while you should have illustrations in mind as you write in order to keep your text sharp and precise, do not give instructions to the artist unless there are ironies or essential, meticulous points that might otherwise be missed. (Does the story come from a certain country? Are there differences in the birds of certain areas, such as the American and English robins? A recent picture book version of *The Twelve Days of Christmas* featured a California quail instead of a partridge in the pear tree. Sloppy illustrating. Sloppy editing.)

A good picture book is fully integrated, story and art, but *the text comes first*. The author of a picture book must remember that dual audience—reader and read-to—tap the emotions of the child waiting within, consider the structure of the 32-page book, and be simple.

The dual audience

The read-tos are the great silent majority of the reading world. They do not purchase manuscripts, edit stories, or even buy finished books. But they can—and will—refuse to listen!

The vocal minority—the ones who buy the books or borrow them from libraries—are the parents, teachers, librarians, grandparents. To reach the children, you have to appeal to the adults first.

Does this sound cynical? It is not meant to be. If you have never been an adult reading a bad ABC book or a simpleminded storybook over and over to your child or children, you cannot know the dark night of the soul when you have to resort to, "Let's watch television," just to be able to put the awful book down.

Some children can stand multiple readings of a bland or uninteresting or sentimental book because of the cuddling they associate with it. Reading is, after all, tactile entertainment, exciting more than just to the ear and eye. A child craving laptime might just as readily listen to a complete rendition of the Brooklyn telephone book. Or perhaps the child loves a particular book for reasons totally unfathomable to the adult reader: a character reminds him of a favorite teacher; the character has the same name as a best friend; or the mauve color is the exact shade of the child's special blanket. One summer my three-and-a-half year old daughter wanted to hear Alvin Tresselt's *Hide and Seek Fog* twice every night before going to sleep. When the summer was over, so was her fascination for the book. I never knew why—and she was too young to say.

It is not that children as an audience lack critical judgment. They are often quite brutally outspoken, since they have not yet been "civilized" out of twitches, yawns, boos. But to a child a book is more than just a book. It is an integral part of the opening world.

If you want to write good books for children, you must never forget that.

The brain is a narrative device and needs stories.

—Frank Smith

‖ 4

Small Tales, Tall Tales, All Tales

THE PICTURE BOOK, that fusion of illustration and text, begins with the word. So the writer, the tale teller— you—is where the picture book starts.

But there are many different kinds of picture books: storybook, concept book, alphabet and counting books; humorous and serious; rhymed and unrhymed; realistic and fairy tale; nonsense and pedagogical. The range is wide and deep.

One of the most common kinds is the *storybook* that tells a small tale in a few words. Usually, it has a small cast of characters. The typed text normally runs no longer than 10–12 pages, the shorter the better. This is the kind of picture book that really tells a story with a beginning, a middle, and an end. If there is a moral or meaning it is well subsumed by the story.

Yet there is no one kind of storybook. It can be as modern

and realistic as *A Chair for My Mother* by Vera B. Williams, about a poor family who saves their pennies in a jar to buy a much-needed chair for hard-working Mother. It can take place in the past like Brinton Turkle's story of a little Nantucket Quaker lad, *Obadiah the Bold*. The story can be full of modern magic, like Chris Van Allsburg's *The Polar Express;* or an old-fashioned mystery like my *Piggins;* or fairy magic like William Steig's bubbly tale of a donkey, *Sylvester's Magic Pebble.*

In her book of essays, *Down the Rabbit Hole*, Selma Lanes has written of picture storybooks: "The modifier 'literary' is best omitted from this experience, for the contemporary picture book is most clearly understood when viewed as a kind of halfway house between the seductions of TV, film, or the animated cartoon and the less blatant charms of a full page of text." Now certainly the picture storybook has been beaten almost to death by less than literary talents. The "Run Jane Run" school of writing still exists in the minds and hearts of many authors. But the finest picture storybooks are strongly crafted with texts that often have a strong relationship to poetry.

Van Allsburg in *The Polar Express* writes of "cold, dark forests, where lean wolves roamed and white-tailed rabbits hid from our train as it thundered through the quiet wilderness." Wanda Gag in *Millions of Cats* writes that the old man "set out over the hills to look for [a cat]. He climbed over the sunny hills. He trudged through the cool valleys. He walked a long, long time and at last he came to a hill which was quite covered with cats." Alice and Martin Provenson in *The Glorious Flight* write, "Away roars the motorboat. Like a great swan, the beautiful glider rises into the air . . . and shoots down into the river with a splash that frightens the fishes."

These are three very different picture storybooks: (1) a

kind of Christmas dream; (2) folk tale; and (3) historical anecdote. But they are written with poetic instincts, with a rhythmic prose that begs to be read aloud, and with great visual detail. Perfect picture storybook writing and certainly as *literary* as any critic could want.

If you remember that a storybook's text should be a kind of prose poem that must be read aloud, you will see it in perspective. Always read aloud as you write. Listen to the rhythms. You should please the ear as well as the eye. It is only the bad story, the poorly written story, the caption writing instead of story that fits Selma Lanes's harsh description.

Besides a lack of rhythm or visual details, another problem with picture book writing is a lack of tension. A picture book plot should be like a hill with a path leading straight up to the top as the problem (plot) progresses. The high point of the hill is the climax; the end of the book just a short drop down. Too much meandering, and you will lose your young reader. Too many unrelated or stray incidents, and the young listener will wander off. But if *nothing* at all happens, if the problem is solved too easily, before the young reader gets to worry about it or wrestle with it, you may have a soporific—but not a story. The line of the picture book needs to be taut.

Concept Books

The *concept* book, as its name implies, is a book that deals with ideas, concepts, large-scale problems in a small-scale way.

In a sense, concept books are gimmick books. They explore an idea, a concept, in an unusual manner. At their best, they do it in a manner that will both teach and amuse.

To write a concept book, you must first come up with an idea: what is time? what is rain like? what can you do with a rock? where do animals sleep? what are good manners? what are snow and fog? Of course, there probably have already been concept books written about these ideas before. You can find out by checking in the subject index of *Books in Print* in the library.

You will find that Phyllis McGinley did a book about time in rhyme. That Uri Shulevitz's *Rain Rain Rivers* deals with precipitation in a tone poem. Byrd Baylor's poetic picture book text says: "Everybody/needs/a rock./I'm sorry for kids/who don't have/a rock/for a friend." In *Where Do Bears Sleep?* by Barbara Shook Hazen, a child can learn that animals sleep in pens and dens, in caves, on rafters, rooftops, and in holes, among other places. No one has yet written a more delightful manners-for-little-kids book than Sesyle Joslin's *What Do You Say, Dear?* or the follow-up *What Do You Do, Dear?* And Alvin Tresselt's prose poems *White Snow, Bright Snow* and *Hide and Seek Fog*, with Roger Duvoisin's glowing pictures, are already classics of children's literature.

But just because an idea has already been explored by one writer in a concept book does not put it off limits to others. As there are supposed to be only ten basic plots, so there are probably a finite number of concept book ideas that appeal to young readers. What will make your concept book original is the handling of the idea.

Different ways of approaching a concept might be:

- in rhyme like Barbara Shook Hazen's *Where Do Bears Sleep?*
- in occasional rhyme like Eve Merriam's *Small Fry*
- in question/answer format like Sesyle Joslin's manners books
- in a prose poem like Byrd Baylor's *Everybody Needs A Rock*

- in story form like Marcia Brown's *Once A Mouse*
- in cartoon captions like *When the Wind Blows* by Raymond Briggs

The same concept done by different authors can be startlingly different. Four books that explore that childhood favorite big/little demonstrate this easily: Leonore Klein's *Tom and the Small Ant*, Kazue Mizamura's *The Way of an Ant*, Marcia Brown's *Once A Mouse*, and my book *It All Depends*. The Klein book and my book are both in occasional rhyme alternating with rhythmic prose. The Mizamura and Brown books are straight stories. The former is a more didactic tale about an ant that keeps climbing higher and higher—first on flowers, then on trees—in an attempt to reach the sky. The latter is a very spare, stark fable based on an Indian folk tale, about a hermit and a mouse. As distinct as the four books are, each explores the same basic idea: what is big, what is little?

Again, we can see how differently authors approach the same topic in five books about war: *Hiroshima No Pika* (Toshi Moruki); *When the Wind Blows* (Raymond Briggs); *Rose Blanche* (Roberto Innocente and Christophe Galaz); *Potatoes, Potatoes* (Anita Lobel); and *The Minstrel and the Mountain* (Jane Yolen).

Toshi Moruki's brutally honest book about the dropping of the bomb on Hiroshima follows a young girl Mii and her mother at the fatal moment: "Mii watched as her mother examined her father. 'He's hurt badly,' she said. She untied the sash from her kimono and wrapped it around her husband's body as a bandage. Then she did something amazing. She lifted him onto her back and, taking Mii by the hand, started running." By contrast, *When the Wind Blows* is almost playful in its cartoon-strip depiction of a British husband and wife after the H-bomb falls. *Rose Blanche* is an understated and almost unbearably moving book about the concentration camps where a little Aryan girl watching from outside the barbed wire does not quite understand what is going on in there. All three books need explanations by an adult along with the reading. *Potatoes, Potatoes* is a modern folk tale about a mother who manages to stop a war by feeding all the young soldiers. And *The Minstrel and the Mountain* is a fable about a minstrel who solves a war between two look-alike kingdoms by getting them to exchange places. Five totally different books about the concept of war.

Concept books really began with Margaret Wise Brown, author of the classic *Goodnight, Moon,* who in the 1930s began writing what have been called "awareness compositions." Brown launched a seemingly endless line of these perception books. Her imitators became legion. By the 1950s, with schools and libraries demanding more and more of such primary education books, "It began to look," wrote educator May Hill Arbuthnot, "as if we were in for a kind of pernicious anemia of theme and plot, with language experience in place of stories, and pitter-patter in place of events."

The anemia has cleared up. The concept books being demanded today must be full-bodied texts, not just the pitter-patter educational experiences, though the ghost of those books exists in the baby board books that enjoyed a vogue at the beginning of the 1980s baby boomlet.

The demand comes from editors, librarians, parents— and children, too—because these books explore something worth exploring. It gives the child reader a handle on a particular idea. The concept book is a child's mnemonic device. Conscious language play and idea play for children at the moment when play and learning intersect so completely.

Therefore, besides just coming up with a strong idea/

concept and an original approach, the writer of the concept book must remember that the book must be fun or amusing or fascinating or provocative. The straightforward didacticism of an old-fashioned textbook is to be avoided at all cost. The smarmy, cute condescension of a Sunday School text must likewise be shunned. Also rhyme, unless handled extremely well, degenerates too quickly into doggerel. Just because Dr. Seuss can write a book about war in rollicking rhyme—*The Butter Battle Book*—and get away with it should not be taken as an open invitation to others. Rhythmic prose or occasional rhymes are usually much more effective.

A concept book sticks to a simple idea and expands upon it. In music this is known as a "riff" or "variations on a theme." Concept books are riff books. You should embroider the original idea, play with it, have a good time. But do not stray from one simple idea to another simple idea. That suddenly makes a simple concept book much too complex to work.

Other concept books to look at if you are considering writing this type of picture book are Wendy Watson's *Has Winter Come?*, Ann Turner's *Dakota Dugout*, Charlotte Zolotow's *My Grandson Lew*, Barbara Berger's *Grandfather Twilight*, Nancy Carlstrom's *Wild, Wild Sunflower Child, Anna*, Ianthe Thomas' *Lordy, Aunt Hattie*, Cynthia Rylant's *When I Was Young in the Mountains*.

The concept book will probably be shorter in manuscript than a picture storybook. While the picture storybook runs slightly over ten pages, a concept book should remain below ten. My *Ring of Earth* was seven typed pages, not all of them full. *It All Depends* was shorter. I have seen excellent concept book manuscripts of less than a page: Sendak's *Where the Wild Things Are*, Barbara Berger's *Grandfather Twilight*, Uri Shulevitz's *Dawn*.

ALPHABET BOOKS

The type of picture book that seems to be the easiest to write but is probably the single most difficult to write well is the alphabet book. Writing it is not as simple as ABC.

I have attempted any number of alphabet books. My very first children's book (never sold) was an ABC of girls' names and its companion ABC of boys' names. I have also tried an urban ABC, a pirate ABC, a famous kings and queens ABC, and a new mother's ABC. (D was for diapers, of course.)

Most were dismal. F for failures.

As an editor, I read at least twenty attempts at alphabet books a month since it is the kind of picture book most often tried by novice writers. But professionals have also written poor ABCs. As a book reviewer, I've seen published alphabet books that fall well below acceptable standards.

From the 1800s version of *A-Apple Pie* by Kate Greenaway, through Edward Lear's funny phonetic nonsense alphabet, Wanda Gág's *ABC Bunny*, Garth Williams' charming *Big Golden Animal ABC* to the wildly colorful *Wildsmith's ABC*, the magnificent stateliness of Margaret Musgrove's *Ashanti to Zulu* and the brilliant wordless play of Mitsumasa Anno's *Anno's Alphabet*, the best authors and illustrators have tried their hands at such books. Yet a great many of them fail because the alphabet book is an anomaly. The authors are trying to teach the ABCs, yet they must use as the tool of teaching the very thing they are trying to teach. It is a puzzle.

Alphabet books are enduring and popular because they seem the perfect beginning book for very young children as yet unable to read: a book and a lesson rolled into one. Yet most of them are much too sophisticated in both concept and development for the very young pre-reader to understand.

The simplest of the ABC books—and to many minds the best—are the ones that show the letters of the alphabet clearly and a single, easy-to-identify object beginning with the letter: *A* for *apple*, *B* for *ball*. In Bert Kitchen's strongly original *Animal Alphabet*, for example, the letter B has two bats hanging from the top and middle bars of the letter; the letter E is pushed by an enormous and meticulously painted elephant. But there is no need for a writer for this kind of book. The artist's interpretation of each object associated with a letter provides the book's distinction. However, Kitchen's exquisitely rendered drawings do not overcome what is every alphabet book's main problem: the ease with which an unlettered child can identify the object. Kitchen's A is a brown, scaled, clawed animal sitting beneath the central bar of the letter. Is it an anteater? An aardvark? Those were my first guesses. Actually, according to the key at the back of the book (which young children cannot read), the animal is a nine-banded armadillo. How many youngsters would know that?

The writer of an alphabet book is faced with the same problem: After choosing a theme, coming up with enough easy objects for twenty-six letters. Text can often help solve the problem. For example, in Roger Duvoisin's *A for the Ark*, the story of Noah and the animals lining up two by two adds an extra fillip. In Fritz Eichenberg's *Ape in a Cape*, there are odd animals galore, but the rhymes help in identification and add to the fun: "Goat in a boat" and "Fox in a box." In Phyllis McGinley's *All Around the Town*, the sprightly verses wittily combine letters and sounds: "V is for the vendor, a very vocal man."

You might try your own version of these, or any of the following: a hospital ABC; things-on-wheels ABC; a Halloween ABC (*G* for *ghost*, *W* for *witch*, *B* for *broomstick* and *black cat*, *J* for *jack-o'-lantern*, etc.). You might try a garden ABC, a woodland animals ABC, an insect ABC, a country music/city mouse ABC. You might write it in prose, in captions, in rhyme. Or there might be a story attached.

The children's room of your local library is a repository of themes tried and definitely the place to visit before attempting to develop your own alphabet theme. First, give your ABC book idea a thorough library test. There is nothing more discouraging or embarrassing than a rejection letter that says: "Alas, we feel this delightful book is too similar to. . . ."

Once you have an original theme, give your idea the *X test*. Since an alphabet book stands or falls on its most difficult letters (usually *X*, *J*, *Q* and *Z*), it is imperative that you find out what you can do with them before going ahead with the project. In the abortive pirate alphabet book I tried, *X* happened to be easy. It stood for the spot marked on the treasure map. *J* was for *jewels*. But I never did find an object for *Z*.

If the *X* or *Q* or *J* or *Z* is only vaguely recognizable or only tangentially related to the theme, find a better one or forget about the project.

I once had a perfectly marvelous idea for an alphabet book: *A, B, A Building I See*. It was about the building of a skyscraper, each letter demonstrating a step in the process. It began:

A is for architect,
   he is the man
   who begins the new building
   by making a plan.
     He begins the building the way A begins the alphabet.

I got all the way through the book, writing little verses for each letter, until I got to X. I even had a brilliant idea for that one: X marks the new panes of glass to keep people from putting their hands through the windows. I consulted my cousin, a New York City architect who told me more than I wanted to know about the entire process of constructing a building. However, I never made sure I had something for each letter before I began. I just plunged in with A and worked my way along, spending weeks polishing each little gemlike verse. I even sent my cousin an expensive bottle of his favorite liquor in thanks. And then, several months later, I landed on Y and Z and—oops. All I could come up with was, Y is for *yardstick* and Z is for *Zinc* with which the girders (already enclosed by this part of the book) are dusted. Suggestions from friends and acquaintances and well-meaning strangers who heard me mention the problem in speeches ranged from "Y is for *Yippppeee, the building is finished*" to "ZZZZZZZZZ, *the architect is asleep.*"

I never sold the book.

It was after my fifteenth or twentieth rejection that I devised the *X Test.*

An alphabet book may be in rhyme or prose. It may be straightforward, nonsensical, or outrageously silly. It may be informative (*Ashanti to Zulu* is encyclopedic in its attention to African tribes) or it may seek only to entertain. It may be illustrated with drawings, paintings, watercolors, magic marker, scratchboard, photographs or any other artistic medium. But as with all picture books, it must be simple. It is a book for non-readers.

There are a number of published ABC books that are not simple, using enormous words and complicated actions: Dahlov Ipcar's *I Love My Anteater with an A*, Peggy Parish's *A Beastly Circus*, Barbara Wersba's *Twenty-Six Starlings Will Fly Through Your Mind*. These books use works like "xenophobia" and names like "Xerxes" or

"Xanthippe," or say elegant and mysterious things like "P, the proud cat/ is sister to Q/ and they quarrel/ through centuries of prose./ Their arguments range/from the price of a pin/to the possible qualms of a quail." They simply beg the alphabet book question. They are not for children at all. They are for adults.

COUNTING BOOKS

Less popular with authors but just as important for a child's development are books that present numbers. Usually these books deal with numerals 1 through 10, though occasionally they group objects by fives and tens.

As with alphabet books, counting books are most successful when they are simple.

Sometimes additional information, story, or rhyme adds to the fun. *Moja Means One*, a Swahili counting book by Muriel and Tom Feelings is such a book. My counting rhyme *An Invitation to the Butterfly Ball*, with its little animals scrambling for party clothes, another.

Any writer of counting books should keep in mind, though, that these are books for children, not adults. You must rein in any tendency to be too broad, too cute, too ironic, or too abstract. Writing "One is for the All, the Great Whole, the Singularity we feel" may reflect your personal theology, but not only is it impossible to illustrate, it is self-indulgent. A counting book is supposed to help familiarize children with the shapes of numbers and their relationship to counting. If the book does not do that, then, it simply is not a good book for children.

Tales are, in the ears of their hearers, permissible lies.

　　　　　　　　—Roger D. Abrahams

‖ 5

We Are Story

ONCE UPON A TIME, of course, there were no written stories, no literary or art tales. But there were bits and pieces of legend, myth, history all twined together and transmitted orally from father to son, mother to daughter. This way of preserving folk history has been called "a process of mouth-to-mouth resuscitation."

The invention of the alphabet changed all that. Slowly all the tales were set down on rock or parchment or paper—whatever was handy at the time. By taking these fluid, ever-changing, ever-adapting tales out of the mouths of tellers and putting them down in a more permanent form, story writers changed the stories forever. People began to believe that what was written was so, and, conversely, what was not written was not so.

In many ways we still believe that what is written down is so. An argument ends when someone quotes *Time* or *Newsweek* or *The New York Times* in exactly the way our forefathers quoted scripture. Sometimes it is difficult to find the kernel of truth that began the stories.

Where stories began

It is the same with folk tales. Within each of those old stories is a kernel of truth. If you are a scholar and want to delve into the who-is the-real-King-Arthur controversies or what-was-a-dragon-really or were-the-Picts-the-precursors-of-the-faerie-folk or did-dugongs-start-the-mermaid-stories, that is your prerogative. However, it is not necessary to the writing of successful fairy and folk tales to know *what* began the old stories; it is only necessary to know that a distorted or slanted truth was most often the beginning point. As Dennis the Menace says to his father in a cartoon: "I didn't fib! I made a *fable* like Aesop and those other guys."

The old stories were told for and by people who, in William Butler Yeats's phrase, "steeped everything in the heart; to whom everything was a symbol." He was talking about a peasant class. But the people these tales appeal to most today are the young readers and those of us who, like the children, still have everything steeped in the heart. We—the children and the childlike—look at a dugong and see a mermaid, glimpse a moth at dusk and see a newly-released soul, look at dinosaur bones and read dragon, and count all windmills as giants.

To write stories in the folk tale tradition involves a process I call *mining the folk lode*. The writer has to draw upon the old sources either consciously or unconsciously, recreating subtly the atmosphere where these stories would have been told: around the campfire, in the great halls, or in the nursery. As a writer, you may use the folk wisdom of the fantastics and fools, the giants and dragons, the elves and fairies that once peopled the countryside of humankind's mind. You may restructure an old song, weaving the elements into a new story-tapestry. Or you may simply, like the peasant nanny telling tales to her charges, recall an old tale heard in childhood, working your own special magic and voice on the material. (This last is what scholars like to call "the folk process at work.") But you must begin with a basic love of the ancient stories, approaching them with respect and that sense of wonder I mentioned before.

The nanny tales

These are the dear familiar stories you may have learned directly from your parents' own storehouse of stories or from the pages of a worn and well-beloved book. Sometimes called "cottage tales" or "household tales," they can be found in many different versions (or "variants," as folklorists call them). Stories like "Sleeping Beauty," "Jack the Giant Killer," "Little Red Ridinghood."

For example, "Cinderella" has been traced by scholars from China to Peru, with many stops in between. An early study noted some five hundred variants in Europe alone—which gives you a good idea how often a basic story can be changed. In the English version, "Catskin," the girl manages to get dresses made of silver, gold, and feathers to entice her prince, but finally wins him through her wits. The Scottish Cinderella is "Rushen Coatie" and her slipper, though capable of jumping into the prince's pocket by itself, is of good serviceable leather. The glass slipper is the French fairy tale writer Charles Perrault's invention, created in the 17th century along with the fairy godmother and the midnight warning. It was probably a mistake in translation. The French word *vair* means fur, and the sound-alike word *verre* means glass. Somewhere along the way the two words were confused. Mouth-to-ear-to-pen is a very noisy channel. Something was lost, and something more was gained when the story went from an oral to a written form.

Retelling an old story is, from a writer's point of view, the simplest use of folk material; yet it is not so simple if you wish to do it well. If you are particularly in love with an old tale and want to set it down in a beautiful new form, or if you are an artist wanting to create new pictures and you need a sprightly new telling to go along with your visualization, then you must begin with as many of the old sources as you can find.

If you are interested in the wide range of these old tales, at least some to the following books should be on your shelves: *Irish Fairy and Folk Tales* (William Butler Yeats), as well as *Irish Folk Tales* (Henry Glassie); a good translation of *Grimm's Fairy Tales* (and there are many); the Lady Charlotte Guest's classic retelling of the Welsh hero tales, *The Mabinogion*. Also *British Folktales* (Katherine Briggs); *Norwegian Folk Tales* (Peter Asbjoernsen and Jorgen Moe); *Russian Fairy Tales* (Afanas'ev); *The Golden Bough* (Sir James George Frazer); *The White Goddess* (Robert Graves); the four volume *The Masks of God* (Joseph Campbell); a translation of *A Thousand and One Nights;* *African Folktales* (Roger D. Abrahams); *American Indian Myths and Legends* (Richard Erdoes and Alfonso Ortiz); *Jewish Stories One Generation Tells Another* (Penina Schramm); *Chinese Fairy Tales and Fantasies* (Moss Roberts); *The Book of Negro Folklore* (Langston Hughes and Arna Bontemps); *Arab Folktales* (Thea Bushnaq); and the five volume *English and Scottish Popular Ballads* (Sir Francis James Child).

The older versions of the stories are often closer to the oral tradition from which these tales sprang, though certain retellers (Sir Walter Scott, Charles Perrault, even the Brothers Grimm) took liberties with the tales, adding here and subtracting there to set down wonderful stories. But often the collectors took these stories straight from the mouths of the tellers. As you read them, you will note at once the poetic folk style. These are stories meant (like children's books) to be told aloud. The word *tale* comes from the Anglo-Saxon *talu* or speech. Tale is related to telling. So the tale as it is retold on the page should still be pleasing to the ear.

Read each of your sentences out loud as you write. Pretend you are telling the story to eager listeners. Then the tale will have that folk quality of mouth-to-ear. Sound is the vital element. Said C.S. Lewis: "It is important to please the ear as well as the eye."

Here are the openings to three versions of a famous British folk tale. The first is from folklorist Katharine Briggs's *British Folktales*, though taken from a much older source. The second is from a Joseph Jacobs version first printed in 1898. The third is from a modern retelling. All three have wonderful poetry in them, but a different style, a different voice, and a completely different character. Good poetry makes good drama. The best tales are full of both.

From the Briggs:

> Constant tradition says that there lived in former times in Soffham [Swaffham] alias Sopham in Norfolk, a certain pedlar, who dreamed that if he went to London Bridge, and stood there he should hear very joyful newse. . . .

From the Joseph Jacobs version:

> In the old days, when London Bridge was lined with shops from one end to the other, and salmon swam under the arches, there lived at Swaffham in Norfolk, a poor pedlar. He'd much ado to make his living, trudging about with his pack at his back and his dog at his heels, and at the close of the day's labour was but too glad to sit down and sleep. Now it fell out that one night he dreamed a dream, and therein he saw the great bridge of

London town, and it sounded in his ears that if he went there he should hear joyful news.

And from *The Pedlar of Swaffham,* a picture storybook by Kevin Crossley-Holland:

> One night John Chapman had a dream.
> A man stood by him, dressed in a surcoat as red as blood; and the man said, "Go to London Bridge. Go and be quick. Go, good will come of it."

To do more than just a gimmicky job, the dedicated reteller should have some idea of the background of a legend or tale. Crossley-Holland knew what a man of the time—even in a dream—would be wearing. *A surcoat.* Jacobs could say in a few phrases what a pedlar would look like. None of those is in the oldest source. These writers did their homework. Just as an illustrator of a tale has to know costume and landscape, the writer should have such knowledge.

Barbara Cooney, when she retold and illustrated Chaucer's *Chanticleer and the Fox,* drew a raven sitting in one of the windows because in Chaucer's day a raven was an omen of ill-to-come. All the flowers she drew lovingly in the book grew in England when Chaucer was alive. She has written of the book that she did not expect every child—or even every adult—to "get" those touches. But they help create a total world. If an illustrator takes that much time with a book, surely the author must, too.

Does this sound like too much work when all you wanted to do was simply retell an old folk tale? Books, even picture books, change lives. When you think of it that way, asking the author to do a little bit of homework is not asking too much.

Great Hall stories

In the once-upon-a-time days, the nobles and their ladies would listen to a wandering minstrel or troubador sing of great deeds, of quests, dragons conquered, battles fought, maidens won. The modern writer can, like J.R.R. Tolkien, Lloyd Alexander, Robin McKinley, or Patricia McKillip borrow these bardic elements and reshape them to his own use.

Tolkien, for example, made up Hobbits and Ents. But he borrowed Trolls and Elves. Yet in the process—the *folk process*—he gave back more than he took. His Lothlorien will forever be the place of elvish enchantment to anyone who reads *The Lord of the Rings*. Dragons will always sound a little like Tolkien's greedy Smaug in *The Hobbit*. Lloyd Alexander may have leaned heavily on the Welsh *Mabinogion* for his Prydain books, but he created an Assistant Pigkeeper who will ride forever in the reader's mind like a lantern bearer for the older gods.

These Great Hall stories are usually quest tales in which a hero or heroine moves through one magical adventure after another in search of reward or a boon to bring back to the kingdom. As such, these stories usually need a larger scope than a picture book can offer. Novel length is preferable and will be discussed later in the chapter on fantasy.

However, the line between folk tale and fantasy is a fine one, crossed and recrossed at will. And certainly there are some times a Great Hall tale can be told in the small form: *Everyone Knows What A Dragon Looks Like* by Jay Williams is one that is successful. As is *Helga's Dowry* by Tomie de Paola, a troll tale; *Jim and the Beanstalk* by Raymond Briggs, a satirical giant story; and my own *Dove Isabeau*. The difference is that these stories miniaturize the Great Hall adventure, focusing on a single element in what could easily be opened up into a larger book.

Campfire tales

So we come to the great catch-all, the campfire tale, of which there are many kinds.

First are the *cumulative stories* like "The House That Jack Built," which first spiral upward and then back downward to a conclusion. Other cumulative stories are "The Gingerbread Man" and "Henny Penny" and the prize-winning book by Don and Audrey Woods, *The Napping House.*

These stories work marvelously with the very youngest listeners. The endless repetitions and the utter simplicity of the story line catch and hold even the most inattentive youngsters until they find themselves telling the story along with the speaker. It is the circular mode of the story that invites participation, just like a round that repeats and repeats. Many of the cumulative stories work right into game situations in the classroom. Yet as simple as this kind of story seems, again it is not. Like canons or rounds which they so closely resemble, they are difficult to work out perfectly. There is a dovetailing that a fine carpenter would envy. Diagraming the story to see if it is "balanced" is helpful.

The second category is the *talking animal tale.* "The Three Bears," "The Three Little Pigs," "Puss in Boots" are good examples from folklore. What these stories have in common—besides the fact that the animals talk—is that they often teach a simple lesson (though by our modern standards the morality of some of the old folktales, like "Puss in Boots," may seem somewhat skewed). But it is dangerous to think in moralistic or didactic terms. Remember what Isaac Bashevis Singer said: "Truth in art that is boring is not true." Talking animal tales are successful only if they are fun to begin with. Read such good modern talking animal stories as Wendy Watson's bedtime story *Has Winter Come?*, Barbara Berger's stately and powerful

Christmas story *The Donkey's Dream*, Munro Leaf and Robert Lawson's classic anti-war parable *The Story of Ferdinand*, and Leo Lionni's patterned *Swimmy*.

You must be extremely careful of the type of story Jean Van Leeuwen once labeled the "Polly Parakeet Ties Her Shoes" story which is neither folk tale nor fantasy. What it is is "cute." It is a kindergarten instruction book using an animal with an alliterative name, overwhelming in its didactic intent, and dripping with honey. Most editors abhor anthropomorphic stories, and they see them every day, especially if they are about defective animals: the bunny who cannot hop, the tiger who cannot roar, the giraffe with the small neck, etc. A good rule of thumb would probably be: If it is an animal, it shouldn't talk; if it is human, it shouldn't walk on all fours. (For more about talking animals, see chapter 10).

However, if despite all warnings you insist on writing a talking animal story, you might try casting it in the folktale mode for—as everyone knows—in the once-upon-a-time days, anything was possible: bears could talk, cats wore boots, and frogs could go a-courting a mouse.

The third category is the *silly tale*. In this type of story, the numbskull or the stupid son (or daughter) does something so outrageous, the reader cannot keep from laughing. There are classic fool stories in folklore: the husband who keeps house; the old man and his son who want to trade their donkey at the fair but cannot figure out how to get it there; the husband and wife who have a bet about who will speak first; the lazy boy Jack who does not know how to bring home his wages from work. Always in the midst of the playful silliness there is a sense of pain. Slipping on a banana peel can look funny, but someone is likely to be hurt. The young reader can feel above this foolishness, can be aware of but not threatened by the pain. And the young reader also feels that he or she is smarter than the ninnies in the story. In the old days, downtrodden peasants made up these tales so that *they* could feel better and smarter than the fools. Children—one of the last of our downtrodden and unliberated minorities—feel the same. And isn't that, in a sense, what much of vaudeville is all about?

Some of the *silly tales* in modern clothes that you might look at before attempting this category of story are Rafe Martin and Ed Young's sprightly *Foolish Rabbit's Big Mistake*; Ann McGovern's *Hee Haw*; and James Marshall's wonderful Stupid stories, such as *The Stupids Step Out*.

In each of these three categories—*cumulative, talking animal,* and *silly tales*—the problem with writing a story "in the manner of a folk tale" or "literary folk tale" or "fakelore" (as the scholars put it), is how to use the device without just paraphrasing an old story.

Here are some ideas you might try:

- a modern setting for "The Gingerbread Man," using a pizza that escapes from the pie baker's hands and rolls out the door and down the street of a modern city. (See also *The Elephant and the Bad Baby* by Elfrida Vipont, an excellent example of the modern use of a cumulative device.)
- three sparrows talk of the coming winter and fly to three separate houses, where they are greeted in three different ways. (See also Mordicai Gerstein's *Arnold of the Ducks*, for a wonderful example of the talking animal tale.)
- a man decides to build a tall apartment building and uses the wrong tool each step of the way, on the advice of his "sidewalk superintendents." (See also Judith Barrett's *Old MacDonald Had An Apartment House*.)

A fourth category of the campfire stories is the *magic tale*: fairies and little people, witches and wizards, wise women and wise men, giants and ogres, magical animals and magical objects. All the trappings of enchantment can be set in a tale. The magic tale is my favorite. The trick is to *borrow* a bit of magic from an old tale and use it in a new way.

In writing *Greyling*, I borrowed the magical being the wer-seal or selchie from Scottish legend but the story told is my own. Hans Christian Andersen borrowed the traditional half-fish, half-woman for his story "The Little Mermaid" but made up both plot and characters. Richard Kennedy used the folk figure of Death, but dressed him up as a modern New England CPA in *Come Again in the Spring*. Jay Williams used the traditional Chinese dragon in his original story *Everyone Knows What A Dragon Looks Like*. It is the use of old images that makes these *folklike*, but the original telling that gives the folk character new life and power.

Some critics of new—and old—fairy tales say that such stories woo children from the real world, giving them the wrong idea about the world in which they live. But I agree wholeheartedly with C.S. Lewis who wrote forcefully: "The fairy tale is accused of giving children a false impression of the world . . . I think no literature gives them less of a false impression . . . What profess to be realistic stories . . . are far more likely to deceive them."

The real and the magical

In writing folk tales as picture books it is important to keep two things in mind. First you must remember that the most unlikely things in modern life may be grist to your mill. Although you may not realize it at the time, elements of real life are always sneaking into the magic.

Here are three examples from my own books and life to illustrate what I mean.

In *The Boy Who Had Wings*, the Greek boy Aetos is never happy when he is different. Only after his wings fall off and he is able to live a "normal" life is he secure. Yet, years later, all the young people in his village pray to the gods and Saint Aetos to send them such "blessed" children, children with great arching wings. It is a story torn from my life. I felt out of place, unappreciated in college, where I was different from other students, with my habit of writing poetry at all hours. Thank goodness *my* wings did not fall off. The story of Aetos is in many ways, a version of my own life.

I began *The Bird of Time*, in which a miller's son discovers a bird that can marvelously control time, the day I was told my mother had inoperable cancer. Ostensibly, the book started when I misheard the lyrics of a rock song on the car radio. Before I had quite caught the real lyrics— which had nothing to do with either a bird or time—I found myself thinking about a time bird. Subconsciously, I was also remembering the *Rubáiyát of Omar Khayyám*, which my mother had given me when I was ten with my favorite lyrics: "The Bird of Time has but a little way/To fly—and Lo! the Bird is on the Wing." I showed my mother the manuscript about six months later (she died before the book was published), and she remarked, "Intimations of mortality, eh?" I realized then what she already understood, that the story was about us. I wanted to be able to slow time down or stop it altogether—the way the hero Pieter does in the book—in order to save my mother. In real life, I could not keep her forever, but in the book I could.

In my picture book *The Girl Who Loved the Wind*, I wrote of a young Persian princess whose father wants to keep her from all the evils of the world, and so he boards her up in a palace and lets no one speak anything but happy thoughts to her. One day the wind leaps in over the wall and tells her that the world outside is not what she thinks, but is both good and bad and ever-changing. In the end, the girl sets her cloak on the ocean water, holds up one end, and is blown out to sea by the wind, toward that ever-changing world, away from the enclosed mansions of her father's heart. It is in a very real way the story of my life, for my own father was extremely overprotective.

So real life informs the literary fairy tale, for we are all types in some of our incarnations: the protected princess, the overprotective father, the adventurous lover, the victim of time, the outcast who dreams of being normal. What translation into the fairy tale mode allows the writer is a kind of mythic shorthand.

Structural elements and techniques

If you remember that anything in your real life can become part of your inspirational mechanism, then you can proceed to the second important point about writing a folk tale: know its structure.

A folk tale manuscript published as a picture book should run between five and fifteen pages, the shorter the better. The age group that most appreciates this kind of tale is 4-104. (Sales people, the most conservative members of a publishing house will tell you that the age of the readers is 4–10). However, as you write, do not worry about either the page or age limitations. Consider those aspects as you revise. But never try to second-guess an editor. I do not—and I am an editor myself!

Some of the structural elements you need to understand are tag-openings, speed of plot, flatness of character, and the creative use of recurring themes or phrases.

Folk tales usually have a tag-opening, like the Persian "Once there was and there was not . . ." You can either use the classic "Once upon a time" or try to create your own opening in a style appropriate to the story. Here are some I have used: "Once on a time when wishes were a-plenty . . ." "Once in the East where the wind blows gently on the bells of the temple . . ." "Once on the far side of yesterday . . ." "Once on the plains of Thessaly where horses grow like wheat in the fields . . ." and "Once upon a maritime . . ." New writers often make the mistake of doubling up on the opening, writing "Once upon a time and a long time ago . . ." because they do not understand that it is simply a device that signals *fairy tale* to the reader.

The theme of this kind of story is usually apparent from its beginning, though there may be subtexts that remain hidden even from the author. This is a story, not a subtle character development or mood piece. The themes are never abstract but are rather robust and easy to understand: earning a place in the world, seeking a fortune, escaping a powerful enemy, outwitting an evil opponent. Or they may be even more specific: marrying the Czar's daughter, getting safely through a dark forest. The subtext, carried over from the author's real life, should never intrude upon the movement of the story but rather play subtly beneath the surface. In *The Boy Who Had Wings*, the theme is Aetos's need to be normal. That the story impinged upon my real life would not be of any interest to the average reader who will bring his or her own needs and life problems to the tale.

Don't waste time in this story. It is so short, you have to compress everything into fewer than fifteen pages. As they say in the modern spy dramas: get in, get it over with, get out. A key phrase to remember when working on such tales is *"and then."* It will remind you of the breathless child at your elbow waiting to hear the rest of the story. In a folk tale speed is of the essence. Speed is helped by an economy of words (keeping the Latinate and polysyllabic words to a minimum), fast action, an inventive plot, and a swift but satisfactory conclusion.

It is important for a folk type story to have a clear and uncluttered end. It does not have to be a happy ending. After all, Andersen's little mermaid dives back into the sea without her prince and minus her tail and her tongue. My Greyling swims away from his loving parents. The girl who has fallen in love with the wind gets blown out to sea away from her father. Aetos loses his wings. But everyone and everything must be dealt with in one way or another. And if this means that the wicked queen must dance in red-hot iron shoes until she drops down dead, as in the classic "Snow White," let her dance. Children want to know that the ends are wrapped up tight. As G. K. Chesterton noted about the Grimm tales, children know themselves to be innocent and so demand justice, but we adults fear ourselves guilty and ask for mercy in our stories.

As for characters, with all that plot and theme, there is not much time for full-bodied, in-depth portrayals. Folk characters tend to be types: foolish son, clever peasant, wise old woman. For the most part, the good are good, the evil evil. One character is rewarded with a handful of diamonds and pearls, the other with a mouthful of toads. Still, small touches can make folktales very individual and make the reader remember them forever. Beauty's absurd longing for a rose in winter delivers her into the hands of the Beast. The third little pig's flat-footed burgher qualities make a house of bricks a totally consistent choice. Such individualizing touches added to the types make up a portrait gallery of unforgettable characters.

Finally, the trademark of folk tales is the recurring phrases or themes. It is important to remember the famous "rule of three," in which three is the magic number (three little pigs; three magic wishes; three adventures; three brothers; a road to the left, a road to the right, and a road in the middle). Often a little rhyme or catch phrase is repeated ("Fee-fi-fo-fum, I smell the blood of an Englishman"). It is a signal to the young reader that is clear as punctuation.

Why write new stories

That leaves only one question to be answered. With all the delightful, powerful, unforgettable stories already in the oral tradition and the tales already transcribed by such authors as Charles Perrault, why write new, original ones?

Folk tales and fairy stories carry important messages to the conscious, the pre-conscious, and the unconscious mind. The noted child psychologist Bruno Bettleheim in his fascinating book *The Uses of Enchantment: The Meaning and Importance of Fairy Tales,* wrote, ". . . they offer new dimensions to the child's imagination, suggesting to him images with which he can structure his daydreams."

Fairy tales are important. The old ones remind us how we still dream the same dreams as our ancestors did. The new ones make modern what might be too ancient to be understood as originally told or add to the vocabulary of those dreams.

If the new stories are well told, they can be as valid as the old. The children are heirs to all three traditions: the oral, the retold or transcribed, and the literary or new tales. They do not distinguish between the origins for their enjoyment. As May Hill Arbuthnot, the great chronicler of the history of children's literature wrote: "The distinction between the old folk tale and the modern fairy tale is of no importance to the child. Magic is magic to him, whether he finds it in Grimm, Andersen, or Dr. Seuss."

*Realize that what grows out of imagination
has to become words first to become a poem*
                                    —Harry Behn

‖ 6

Ma Goose and Her Goslings

THE CHILD'S FIRST LITERATURE is poetry. Children seem to make rhymes before they make words. They respond to musical language and the tra-la-las and rhythmic finger games like "This Little Piggie Went To Market," before they can competently follow the logic of stories. The nursery rhymes, whether by Mother Goose or A. A. Milne, become childhood mantras to them, carried along into adulthood with a surer recall than almost anything else.

But it is a mistake to think that all poetry is for young children. Or that all rhyme is appropriate for toddlers and tots. Or that poetry without end rhyme cannot be loved by the little ones.

The mistaken assumption that little rhymes are only for little children comes from the fact that the reigning monarch in the nursery has long been Mother Goose. Perfect rhymes—words that rhyme exactly—like "Jack and Jill/ Went up the hill"—sit comfortably and familiarly on the ear.

But they are not the only types of rhyme in the nursery canon.

There are near rhymes (thought by some to be "bad" rhymes) like "Fee-fi-fo-fum/I smell the blood of an Englishman." There are made-up names or words just to complete a rhyme like "Little Nanny Etticoat/In her white Petticoat." There are identical rhymes, with deliberate repetition of a word or phrase:

> This is the way the farmer rides,
> The farmer rides, the farmer rides.
> This is the way the farmer rides
> So early in the morning.

Here the lines depend upon rhythm alone for their power.

As Eve Merriam, a contemporary poet who often writes for children, puts it:

> It doesn't always have to rhyme,
> but there's the repeat of a beat, somewhere
> an inner chime that makes you want to
> tap your feet . . .

Mother Goose

As simple as Mother Goose rhymes appear to be, and as appropriate for the youngest listeners, many of these old favorites have their roots buried in mythology's past or in street-corner polemics. "Little Jack Horner," for example, was written at the time of Henry VIII's dissolution of the monasteries. Mr. Horner was Thomas Horner, steward to the last of the abbots of Glastonbury Cathedral. The abbot sent Horner to London with a Christmas gift for the king—a pie in which the deeds to twelve manorial estates had been baked. Horner stuck in his hand and lifted out the plum of all these deeds and kept it for himself. The abbot was hanged, beheaded, and quartered for cheating the monarch. The Manor of Mells, a fine plum of an estate, is still in the hands of Horner's descendants.

Other so-called simple nursery rhymes record similar street corner tattle-taling, folk wisdom, weather chants, or herdsmen's counting rhymes, such as "Hickory Dickory Dock." One rhyme may even (scholars argue the point) warn of the symptoms of the plague—"Ring-a-ring-o' roses."

And some still keep the account of terrible racist name-callings:

> Taffy is a Welshman,
> Taffy is a thief,
> Taffy came to our house
> And stole a leg of beef . . .

is not a rhyme to recite on vacation in Wales.

Poets for children today would not want to emulate the nursery rhyme physical abuse ("I took him by the left leg/ And threw him down the stairs"), or the brutal deaths ("All the king's horses/ And all the king's men/ Couldn't put Humpty/ Together again") or the racial slurs. And yet today, among the most popular of children's poets are Shel Silverstein and Jack Prelutsky, who chronicle the same kind of improbable events, horrifying deaths, and skewed morality as the nursery rhymes. For example, Silverstein talks about the snail that lives inside your nose and will bite your finger off if you put your finger in your nose. And Prelutsky's book *Nightmares* includes, among other scary creatures, a ghoul who delights in eating children finger by finger. Neither of them, however, includes racial slurs in his poems.

What makes Mother Goose and, by extension, the kind of light verse written by the Silversteins and Prelutskys, still popular today is the simplicity of language, the directness of the rhyme, the incredible visual appeal of the poems, and a lot of whacky, anarchic humor. Often, there are easy-to-repeat refrains or traveling lines that pop up over and over again. Many of the poems are fast-paced little stories in rhyme. And even the more sophisticated readers in fourth, fifth, and sixth grades find the defiant humor to their taste.

Nonsense poetry

There are basically seven kinds of poems for children: *nonsense, rhymed humor, unrhymed humor, serious rhymed, serious unrhymed, occasional rhymed,* and *prose poems.* Some poets writing today have the ability to straddle the serious and the humorous, even within a single poem. David McCord, Eve Merriam, and Mary Ann Hoberman are singularly adept at such transitions.

Nonsense poems can be traced back to those la-la-la refrains in folk songs and folk rhymes, though what some of us now call nonsense may at one time have made a lot of sense. For example: "Eeeny meeny miny mo" and "hickory dickory dock" are related to counting syllables used by Welsh and Irish shepherds in the fields who, unable to do arithmetic, devised their own counting systems to keep track of their flocks.

A nonsense poem is inventive in both theme and words. It is inspired incongruity. Unlike ordinary light verse, its charm depends upon absurdity—either of situation, character, or language.

The great acknowledged master of the nonsense poem was Edward Lear, and his favorite rhyme scheme was the limerick (some say it was his invention). Actually, limericks began in the late 1830s with young Victoria on the throne. Ladies and gentlemen passed social evenings improvising comic verse, and after each four-line absurdity, appending a fifth line which was always the same: "Will you come up to

Limerick?" (Any reference to Ireland in those days was sure to bring down the house!) Lear wrote hundreds of limericks, and other nonsense verse, including the inspired "The Owl and the Pussy-cat."

Today school children often attempt limericks in class as an exercise, but the form is not much in favor except for an occasional rhyme by modern nonsense poets like N. M. Bodecker. Writers who want to write nonsense verse for children should read such verse attentively, and be warned that *good nonsense* is extremely difficult.

First, the poem must have its own internal and irrefutable logic. Dr. Seuss's *The Cat in the Hat*, for example, leads children on to more and more absurd adventures, but the ending sets things aright. Lear's "The Owl and the Pussy-cat" do what they do because they have fallen in love. Lewis Carroll's Father William's antics are all within the crazy logic of "being old"; his "Jabberwocky" is frightening even without a glance at the Tenniel drawing.

Second, the nonsense poem, for all that it *seems* to go in any direction it wishes, is quite tightly structured. No extra flourishes, no extra syllabification. Each nonsensical act leads to something else. In other words, nonsense is *not* random, but carefully planned.

Humorous poems

Humor is not, of course, confined to nonsense, nor is it confined to rhyme, though in fact there is a tension that rhymed poetry brings with it, an expectation of what the final rhymed word will be, that often makes humor work.

When we hear:

The Troll to Her Children

Billy Goat Gruff
Was yesterday's lunch,
So go to sleep fast
Or I'll give you a . . .

the anticipating child can supply the word *punch* and delights in being part of the rhyme-making.

But there are other ways, besides straight anticipation, to make humor work in poems.

1. Making up new words, the way Lear, Seuss, or Lewis Carroll have done:

Jabberwocky

'Twas brillig and the slithey toves
Did gyre and gimbel in the wabe:
All mimsy were the borogoves
And the mome raths outgrabe.

"Beware the Jabberwock, my son!
The jaws that bite, the claws that catch!
Beware the Jubjub bird, and shun
The frumious Bandersnatch!"

When a poem is truly successful, chockablock full of such nonsensical words, phrases, characters, the lines actually seem to be making sense. Carroll's genius was such that a good many of his made-up words have become accepted as part of the literate person's vocabulary.

2. Using contractions or new spellings of words just for the sake of silliness can add to the element of surprise. Masters of this are Hilaire Belloc, Ogden Nash, and N. M. Bodecker. Here is a small poem by Belloc as an example:

---

*"The Troll to Her Children" by Jane Yolen, from *Dragon Night* (Methuen, 1981).
**"Jabberwocky" by Lewis Carroll, from *Through the Looking Glass*.

The Hippopotamus

I shoot the hippopotamus
with bullets made of platinum,
Because if I use leaden ones
his hide is sure to flatten 'em.

And in the same vein, one of my own poems:

Laurel Tree

If Apollo hadn't chased Daphne,
We wouldn't haphne.

In the first case, it is a contraction that makes the rhyme work, and in the second, much like Ogden Nash, it is the surprise of the invented spelling that does it.

3. Brevity in a humorous poem is often the soul of wit. Like a quick one-two punch, what works is the snap of the line. And especially for young people, who hate long poems, such quick wit is appealing.

An example is Bodecker's:

This Life

This life
does some
poor creatures
dirt,
and Mother Nature
lets it;
the early robin
gets the worm,
the early
worm
just gets it.

---

*"The Hippopotamus," by Hilaire Belloc, *The Bad Child's Book of Beasts* (1896).
**"Laurel Tree," by Jane Yolen © 1989.
***"This Life," by N. M. Bodecker, from *PigeonCubes* (Atheneum).

4. Playful language can be very appealing to the young reader. This may include *alliteration*, sometimes called *head rhyme* or *initial rhyme*, in which repeated initial consonants mark the rhyme: "a fair field full of folk." Or *assonance*, a kind of near rhyme, in which the stressed vowels rhyme, but the consonants don't:

> Little Tommy Tucker
> Sang for his supper;
> What shall he eat?
> White bread and butter. . . .

as the old nursery rhyme goes. Or you could make the consonants agree but not the vowels, as in the beginning of this poem from my book, *Best Witches:*

Magic Wands

> When I was young I had a wand
> of willow.
> It was yellow
> and could bend.
> My spells were several
> and rather callow.
> I lent my willow
> to a friend.

While end/friend is a perfect rhyme, it is the anarchy of willow/yellow/callow in the ear that lends the poem its impertinent surprise.

The point is to have fun with the language and the child reader will, too.

At the Witch's Drugstore

> Camel's oil.
> Camomile.

---

*"Magic Wands" and "At the Witch's Drugstore," by Jane Yolen, *Best Witches* (Putnam's, 1989).

Dragon's blood.
Dramamine.
Adder's tongue.
Adhesive tape.
Phoenix feathers.
Phenobarb.
Eye of newt.
Iodine.
Asp venom.
Aspirin.

Just take two
And call the witch doctor
in the morning.

5. Anticipation thwarted is always a good basis for humorous verse. Poems by Shel Silverstein and Ogden Nash are good examples. They play with the reader's inability to keep from jumping ahead of the poet, and shift ground at the last minute, just as in the old camp song "Be Kind To Your Web-Footed Friends":

Be kind to your web-footed friends,
For a duck may be somebody's mother,
Be kind to the citizens of the swamp,
Where the weather is cold and damp,
You may think that this is the end,
But it isn't
          'cause there is another chorus.

Be kind to your friends of the stripe,
For a skunk may be somebody's mother,
Be kind to your friends of the stripe,
Though their odor is often ripe.
You may think that this is the end.
Well—
     it is!

The anticipation is that again there will be another chorus, but when the song/poem says abruptly "it is!" it provokes gales of laughter. Anticipation thwarted.

6. A serious message under the lightness of the verse can also make a smashing poem. Eve Merriam, David Mc-Cord, and Lilian Moore are very successful at this type of verse. Here is one of McCord's most popular poems:

Cocoon
The little caterpillar creeps
Awhile before in silk it sleeps.
It sleeps awhile before it flies,
And flies awhile before it dies.
And that's the end of three good tries.

This profound little poem has only one polysyllabic word—*caterpillar*—and three words with two syllables: *little*, *awhile*, *before*, plus the title "Cocoon." It is extremely simple, repeats its key words over and over for effect, and is the shortest possible route to a deep sentiment about the brevity of life and the importance of trying. There is not a single word wrong; not a fleshy or flashy overblown phrase. A long metaphysical essay might make the point as well. Perhaps not. It is not bumpity-bump verse or ordinary in any way. McCord has invented his own rhyme scheme: AABBB, and the last line is a wonderful surprise, both in its repeating the rhyme and in its phraseology.

Serious poems
Harry Behn, in his wise little book on poetry, *Chrysalis: Concerning Children and Poetry*, wrote, "Not that a poem has to mean anything entirely reasonable, but it should do some of the things we have always thought a poem should do—to waken wonder and delight, to make magic or music, or to call up something beautiful or wise out of a true dream."

Now obviously not all serious poetry for children has had such a mystical intent. The earliest poetry for children was excessively moral and manipulative. There were admonitory verses ranging from:

> Though I am young, yet I may die
> And hasten to Eternity

to the famous John Bunyan rhyme in *A Book for Boys and Girls,* or *Country Rhymes for Children from 1686:*

> The bee goes out and honey home doth bring
> And some who seek that honey find a sting . . .
> Comparison. The bee an emblem truly is of sin,
> Whose sweet, unto a many, death has been.

There is still a great deal of poetry written for children that is didactic, a teaching tool used specifically for a moral or religious purpose, following in the famous footsteps of *The New England Primer:*

> In Adam's fall
> We sinned all.

Also songs on manners, and behavior rhymes. These can be sold to the vast number of religious magazines, but rarely to the major trade publishers or such magazines as *Cricket.*

A number of poets who write mainly for adults have also written occasionally for children: Donald Hall, X. J. Kennedy, Nancy Willard, Norma Farber, Ted Hughes. And one must not forget the many important poets of the past whose work was intended for adults but has been accepted wholeheartedly by children: Emily Dickinson, Robert Frost, Carl Sandburg, William Shakespeare, William Blake, to name a few.

Serious poetry for children has to have a base in simplicity and be about subjects children care about deeply: parents, friendships, fear of the dark, fear of death (which is, after all, what the McCord "Cocoon" is about), school days, pets, specific holidays, sibling rivalry. Such poems should not be about things that have little meaning for children: sexual love or exhaustive metaphoric gamesmanship or a nostalgic look at a field of daisies. Still there are many shocking topics and ideas that a poem for children can touch on, because it may encapsulate emotion familiar to the child, as in this poem from my *Dragon Night:*

Wild Child's Lament
I have no words
Except in dreams.
Awake, I snort and howl.
But when I sleep
The earth herself
Mothers me.
We sing syllables
One to the other
Across the dreamer's world
And so I make
My cautious way,
My animal way,
From sleep to sleep
And, dreaming,
Become a boy again.

A feral child may not be easily accessible to a young child, but the idea of being motherless and lost certainly is. The poem is about that and about a child's inability to explain feelings—"I have no words/Except in dreams" so that even though the subject matter is shocking, the emotion can be understood by the reading child.

All the tools of language available to writers of serious adult poetry are available to those writing poetry for children, but the most important caveat is still: When you write a poem for children, write what would have moved you as a child. Do not recollect nostalgically. Try to reach the child within and let *that* young poet speak.

Occasional rhyme

Both humorous and serious poems can be written in rhyme or in free verse, but sometimes a poem can be even more successful if the two are combined in occasional rhyme, that is, rhymed lines alternating with unrhymed lines.

One of the dangers of tightly rhymed verse is that it sets up a sing-song rhyme that dominates the poem, pulling it in one way or another for the rhyme's sake rather than letting the emotion or theme be the determining force. On the other hand, a danger of so-called free verse is that the poet may sometimes feel too free and forget that the line itself has to have a rhythm, that there is a reason for the line breaks, that nothing is arbitrary. The poem that is written with alternating rhyme and free verse can manage to solve both these problems. It allows the writer the chance to highlight certain sections of a poem with rhyme. It also fools the young reader who doesn't like poetry into believing that the piece is not quite a poem.

Eve Merriam, in her concept book *Small Fry*, concerning the generic names of baby animals, wrote:

> Here comes the cub parade,
> Cubs that doze and cubs that roar.
> > Bear cubs
> > > lion cubs.
> Cubs that flip and cubs that nip.
> Seal cubs
> > shark cubs
> > > tiger cubs

Small Fry, by Eve Merriam (Alfred A. Knopf).

> fox cubs
>
>   leopard cubs
>   otter cubs.

What are not cubs.

See how there is some rhyming *(nip* and *flip)*, and the pounding insistence of the word *cub*, which remind the reader of the generic name and the fact that a variety of very different animals are called *cubs* as babies. And then the final fillip, a wonderful twist: the strange echo of *Otter cubs* and *what are not cubs*, in which the ear insists there is a rhyme though the eye can not find it.

I did a similar thing in my book of four interlocking seasonal poems, *Ring of Earth*. In the section narrated by the Autumn Goose, the poem begins:

> Rise up, rise up, my mate,
> from the chilly land,
> for a rich, warm smell
> as subtle as a poem
> rides the air
> and calls us home.

> Kerhonk. Kerhonk. Kerhonk.

This poem is more traditional than Merriam's, with an actual rhyme of *poem/home* (though jurists could quarrel that the rhyme depends upon mispronouncing "poem"). It is hardly a traditional verse rhyme scheme, however, having two extra lines at the beginning. And the sound of the goose—*Kerhonk. Kerhonk. Kerhonk*—which rhymes with nothing, is repeated at intervals throughout the poem and is the final line, a kind of goose chorus or goose amen.

---

*"Autumn Song of the Goose," by Jane Yolen, from *Ring of Earth* (Harcourt, Brace, Jovanovich, 1986).

Prose poems

Set out in traditional sentences and paragraphs, the prose poem has the rhythmic rise and fall of poetry and the breath spaces of the stanzaic form, but to the eye, it looks nothing like a poem. It is the ear that knows it as a poem. Often a picture book written in prose style can be heard by the careful listener to be a poem. Since picture books—like poetry—beg to be read aloud, it is no wonder this often happens.

An example of this is my picture book *Rainbow Rider*, which begins:

> In the time before time, the Rainbow Rider lived near the edge of the desert by the foot of the painted hills. He was the one who caught the drops of water that occasionally spilled from the desert sky. He was the one who bent them in an arch like his mightly hunting bow. . . .

It has the cadences of a poem, but it is written out like prose.

Sometimes a picture book that is not working as a poem might be recast as prose. The piece will retain the rhythms and perceptions of poetry, yet the book might be more accessible to those young readers who shun poetry.

I did this with my book *Sky Dogs*, about the coming of the horse to the Piegan Indians, which begins:

> My children, you ask how I came to be called He-Who-Love-Horses, for now I sit in the tipi and food must be brought to me and I do not ride the wind. Come close, there, there. Come close and I will tell you.
>
> Once the land winded us, for we had to walk on our own legs from camp to camp, from sky to sky, with only small mangy dogs to carry our rawhide bags and pull the travois sleds.

The grass beneath our feet sang *swee-swash, swee-swash*
and we wore out many moccasins along the paths of the plains.

I think it is easy to see how that was originally a poem,
though in turning it into prose I added the entire first
paragraph, and a closing paragraph as well to bring the
reader back to the time of the old man telling the story.

Publishing poetry

There are basically four ways of selling children's poetry:
singly to a magazine; singly as a book (almost always as a
picture book); in a collection of one's own work; or putting
together a thematic anthology. Each has its own problems—and its own rewards.

Selling single poems is a long, drawn-out process. You
have to become aware of the market. Religious magazines
will have one kind of requirement, more general children's
magazines like *Cricket* or the historical magazine *Cob-
blestones* another. Often, a magazine will send out
guidelines upon request, but you also need to keep an eye
on the informative magazines such as *The Writer* that list
editorial needs and requirements of various publications. It
is always best to look at the magazines first, to get an idea
of the kind of poetry they are publishing. When you submit
a poem to a magazine, make it clear that you are selling
only first rights, and retain all other rights in the poem
after it is published. Children's poetry is often anthologized
over and over again—frequently in well-paying textbooks—
and it's important that you keep the copyright to your
work.

Occasionally, anthologists look for new, previously unpublished poems. Indefatigable anthologists like Myra
Cohn Livingston, Nancy Larrick, and Lee Bennett Hopkins

are always putting together theme anthologies. Though a beginning writer will have a hard time breaking in, writers conferences or ongoing writers workshops, where trade gossip is exchanged, are good places to start. Perhaps you will hear from or about an anthologist who is looking for poems.

A single poem is sometimes marketable as a picture book. Ann Turner's *Dakota Dugout*, Donald Hall's *Ox-Cart Man*, Byrd Baylor's *Everybody Needs a Rock*, my *Owl Moon* are all examples of unrhymed, free-verse poems as single books. Lear's *The Owl and the Pussy-cat* and Dr. Seuss' rollicking stories, such as *Horton Hatches the Egg*, are picture books in rhyme. My *An Invitation to the Butterfly Ball* is a counting rhyme in a single book. There are songs as books (folk songs such as "Froggie Went A-Courtin'" and "The Fox" and pop songs like Livingston Taylor's "I Put My Pajamas On") as well. Everything discussed earlier about picture books applies when trying to write a single poem—rhymed or unrhymed—as a picture book.

Selling a collection of one's own poems usually comes about only after one has considerable success with single sales. While some single-author collections are themeless (unified by the author's reputation as a poet—David Mc-Cord, Lilian Moore, Eve Merriam, Myra Cohn Livingston), most collections by a single author need a theme to tie the poems together. Paul Fleischman's *Joyful Noises* poems are for two voices; Arnold Lobel's *Pigericks* are limericks about pigs; my *Three Bears Rhyme Books* tells of a typical day of the three- or four-year-old (who happens to be Baby Bear); Clyde Watson's *Father Fox's Pennyrhymes* follows the activities of a group of New England fox farmers. Occasionally, a collection includes both stories and poems by a single author, as in my *Neptune Rising* and *The Faery Flag*.

The fourth way of marketing poetry is to select and edit a

thematic anthology with poems by various authors. Don't forget to look at the works of authors like Emily Dickinson, e.e. cummings, Dylan Thomas, Langston Hughes—not normally thought of as poets for children, but many of whose poems are accessible to young readers, especially as part of a thematic anthology. Most poetry anthologies are made up of previously published work: *When the Dark Comes Dancing*, edited by Nancy Larrick and *The Moon's the North Wind's Cooky* by Susan Russo are both very different anthologies of night-time and lullaby poems. Usually the editor/anthologist includes old poems in the public domain along with the more modern poetry. In such a case, the work of the anthologist is two-fold: locating the poems you want to use and then getting the permissions for reprinting them. Sometimes an editor/anthologist will commission well-known poets to write poems on the theme of the specific volume. Michael Patrick Hearn did this for his anthology *Breakfast, Books, and Dreams: A Day in Verse*. One of the two poems I wrote for his anthology, "Homework," has since been anthologized at least a half-dozen times. Sometimes an anthologist will include both previously published and newly-commissioned work. Myra Cohn Livingston does this with her holiday poem series.

A fifth way to market poetry is used so rarely that I mention it only in passing, i.e., to include a poem or two within the body of a longer prose work. Fantasy novels quite often have songs or spells or incantations, such as Tolkien's *Lord of the Rings* trilogy or the poems the little bat makes up in Randall Jarrell's *The Bat Poet*. But even realistic books can have poetry inbedded within. In my *The Stone Silenus*, a young adult book about a girl coming to terms with her father's death and probable suicide, are many bits and pieces and one complete poem because the dead father was a world-famous poet.

A final word

As Rebecca J. Lukens says in her fine *A Critical Handbook of Children's Literature*, the difference between adult and children's poetry "is not in kind but degree." She goes on to delineate what she considers fit matter for children's poems: "Since much of childhood is spent in play, or in wonder at what is common and yet not commonplace, in marveling at what surrounds children in their constantly unfolding world, these are the subjects of children's poetry."

Poetry for children includes tongue twisters and riddles, as well as nonsense rhymes and serious free or rhymed verse. Some of the poems have sharp, well-defined images; some triple-loaded metaphors; and some just nonsensical refrains. It is experience condensed, experience heightened, experience reshaped, revised, and seen anew. Compact intensity—that is what poetry is—whether for children or for adults. But if it is specifically for the child reader, the poet has to experience again with the heart of the child.

The Poet
There is a child
peeking out
behind my eyes,
seeing slantwise,
watching shadows,
finding rainbows
arching over coffee cups,
and angels
scribbling madly
on the heads of pins.

Find *that* child, and you will write poems for children.

---

*"The Poet," by Jane Yolen, © 1989.

It's not good enough to mention they have
tea; you must specify the muffins.
　　　　　　　　—Frances Hodgson Burnett

‖ 7

A Novel Idea

CHILDREN READING NOVELS are reading what editor
Richard Jackson likes to call "discovery fiction." They
are reading to discover things about themselves, to validate
their feelings, and to uncover new ideas about the world.
One could say that about adults reading novels, too, though
adults tend to read to escape rather than discover, to relax
rather than reassess.

There are basically two kinds of novels for young readers,
the middle grade (or middle age) novel for children in late
elementary (4th–6th grade) and YA or young adult (for
children in junior and senior high).

The viewpoint character or the narrator is almost always
a young person, usually a year or two older than the readers for whom the book is intended. Conventional wisdom
states that children will read about children older than they,
but not younger.

Taboo or not taboo

Don't get mired in the belief that there are taboos in children's books. It seems to me there are no taboos left—as long as you use good taste. (And, depending upon your standards, you might say even that has fallen by the wayside.) What was once not even whispered in the parlor, and only snickered at in the barroom, is now legitimate fare for young novel readers. There are novels about drugs (Todd Strasser's *Angel Dust Blues*); about menstruation (Judy Blume's *Are You There God? It's Me, Margaret*); about homosexuality (Isabelle Holland's *The Man Without a Face*); about incest (Elizabeth Winthrop's *A Little Demonstration of Affection*); about child abuse (Willo Davis Roberts' *Don't Hurt Laurie*); about abortion (Norma Klein's *It's Not What You Expect*); about death (Paige Dixon's *May I Cross Your Golden River*); and almost every other once-taboo subject you might name—except, perhaps, bestiality and necrophilia.

The old-fashioned view that certain subjects should be taboo for children simply because they are young is no longer the case. (Though occasionally there are librarians and teachers whose overzealous guardianship of "morals of minors" makes most librarians today blanch, as, for example, when some misguided librarian painted diapers on the little naked boy child in Maurice Sendak's prize-winning picture book *In the Night Kitchen* and wrote to suggest others do the same. Yet, another librarian protested the swearing in Johanna Reiss' Newbery Honor Book, *The Upstairs Room*.)

The reasons subject matter in children's novels has opened up in the last several years are many and varied. But there are basically three factors instrumental in bringing about the change: the development of a classless readership, the rise of the mass media, and especially the advent of television.

Certainly the reading public has changed. Long ago, books were the prerogative of the privileged upper classes; the others had—if they were lucky, and if they could read— the Bible and an occasional chapbook, cheap little folded or sewn together sheets of nursery tales. Most children of the lower classes were too busy on family farms or chained to long days in the factory to read. Now American children at all levels of society are opening books—at least in school— and opening worlds. So as reading became offered to all classes, all classes demanded to see themselves reflected in their books.

Second, the superabundance of magazines of all kinds in supermarkets, newsstands, doctors' offices, bus and train stations, airports, candy stores, etc., has had a lot to do with eliminating the taboos. These magazines and papers are easily accessible to even the youngest children. The headlines scream about drugs, death, and divorce in the same alluring fashion with which the magazine ads tout beauty lotions and beer.

Finally, there is television, with its instant replays of war in the Middle East, terrorist attacks, natural disasters, space fantasies, as well as the explicit sexuality of soap operas and prime time shows. Even a child who does not yet read is exposed to all of these once-taboo subjects on TV.

Pleasing the reader

Author Bruce Coville has said, "Don't pander, but do try to please the child reader." I would add, "And try to stretch him." A child's transition to adult reading really begins with the middle-grade novel. Before that, the child has either been listening to stories or working hard at just learning to read. Novels for middle-grade readers and young adults will have to take into account the same techniques that any novel must: characterization, plot, theme and subtext, and most of all, good writing. But the difference is in appealing to readers of a particular age.

Humor and story are important for these readers. They are not moved by bathos or sentiment or morality unless it is couched in story, and often bolstered by humor. There has to be a great deal of lively dialogue to break up the intimidating blocks of black type.

The slow, leisurely, descriptive books that appealed to children in the past are not popular with today's middle-grade and young adult readers. Used to the swift action in cliff-hanging TV adventures, in which short scenes end with a commercial break, today's young readers like books that also have swift pacing, lots of dialogue, and chapters that end with cliff-hanging suspense.

The middle-grade novel

Shorter than an adult novel (which usually runs 300-plus pages), the middle-grade novel is usually no longer than 150 manuscript pages. Since there are often black-and-white pictures bulking it up, the text doesn't need to be very long.

Often these books begin in the main character's home, a safe jumping-off place for adventure. Popular books like Beverly Cleary's Ramona books (made into a TV series); Judy Blume's many novels; and Patricia MacLachlan's prize-winning *Sarah, Plain and Tall* are typical of such home-based junior novels.

Unlike the picture book, which ranges far afield in time and place, these novels almost always star children ages 8–14, and so an author writing a junior novel should feel comfortable with boys and girls of that age. Dwelling too much on local or topical idioms, fads, and heroes is not a great idea, since fads come and go a lot more quickly than the average book does. You may think a reference to a sports figure or to Michael Jackson, Reebok or Nike running shoes, or to the Cosby show, might give your story pizazz. But it takes an average of two to five years before a book is accepted and published. Five years in the life of a popular culture hero or fad is much too long. Remember the "hula hoop"? The Cabbage Patch doll hysteria? Video games? Expressions like "to the max" and "awesome"? Remember the dodo!

The trick is to get under the skin of a child (the age of the one in your novel), "the metamorphic creature who's showing just enough leg to shed the name of tadpole but who is still hauling around too much tail to qualify for full froghood," in middle-grade author Jerry Spinelli's memorable phrase. The two ways to do this—equally necessary—are to listen to some real, live children and to the child hidden inside of you. Digging back into your memory—mining your past—is invaluable to making a story ring true, as is observation and probing of the present.

The YA novel

When I was a young adult, YA novels did not exist. They came into being about thirty years ago, "invented" by librarians eager to woo teenagers into the library. These novels were designed to appeal to that subset of adulthood still in school, still worried about Saturday night dates, the sock hop, and how to get through junior year in high school without cracking a book.

To parents, television was the apparent and looming enemy, and they hoped the YA novel would restore literature to the adolescent experience.

What the YA novel did at first was to imitate television, reading like a 200-page treatment for a half hour sit-com or an hour-long drama. It metamorphosed in the 1970s into a kind of hospital unit where all sorts of ills were treated: drugs, rape, drinking, divorce, death, sexuality.

Today, the serious problem novel (the one that focuses solely on a serious problem without telling a good story with real characters) is dead, buried by an avalanche of romance novels for the adolescent reader. A good young adult novel today demands that the writer pay attention to story and character first.

Teenagers today are basically conservative. They do not want to be surprised, but validated. They do not want to be preached to, but to find themselves in the novels they read. Surprisingly, they would agree with Virginia's Woolf's dictum that one should "use words that soak up life." They would add, however, *"my life!"*

Characterization

In the junior novel, characterization has to be achieved with short strokes, not long descriptive passages. The young reader does not want to be *told* anything, but to be *shown*. But it is important to include the hero or heroine's name and age fairly early on, so the reader immediately identifies with the main character.

One of the biggest problems with characterization in these novels is consistency. We all are inconsistent in our real lives: one minute a kind and generous mother, the next—almost between heartbeats—grounding a kid with not much more of an explanation than, "Because I'm the mother, that's why!" But a novel, especially a junior novel, cannot have such inconsistent characters. This is art, after all, not real life. In junior novels, an eleven-year-old should act like an eleven-year-old, not like a baby on one page and a grownup on the next. That would confuse the reader. In real life, of course, eleven-year-olds are often just that

inconsistent, changeable, mercurial. But consistency does
not preclude character growth. Not all characters can or
need to grow in the book, but the main character *must*.
There are basically two kinds of characters in a novel: static
and dynamic. The dynamic character is one who is changed
by the situations and events that he experiences.

Selecting the right name is one helpful way to underline
character. If parents are willing to spend days—even
months—trying to come up with a name for a child who will
doubtless change it a half dozen times in school to such
nicknames as Moose, Antsy, Kickapoo, or Pocket Veto (to
name a few of my acquaintances from bygone days), or to
Yule, Heine, and Little Stump, as my own children were
called by their friends, how long should an author take? A
person's name will last only a lifetime. A character's name
will last forever.

Isn't Scarlett O'Hara a wonderful choice for an Irish
spitfire? And it is no coincidence that Romeo and romance
begin with the same syllable. I named the girl in my novel
The Transfigured Hart "Heather Fielding," because she
was an outdoorsy sort of girl, happiest on horseback. I
named the girl in *The Devil's Arithmetic* "Chaya," because
in Hebrew that means "life," and the book takes place in a
concentration camp.

Shakespeare was one of the greatest name-callers in the
literary world: Sir Toby Belch for comic effect; Pease-
blossom, Cobweb, and Mustard Seed for descriptive effect;
Princess Perdita for a lost child. Shakespeare once said,
"What's in a name? That which we call a rose/By any other
name would smell as sweet." Perhaps. But if Toby Belch
had been the name of Juliet's one true love, I am not so
sure!

Just as a name can help you establish a character in the
reader's mind, a "tag" for that character will make the

assocation that much more vivid. A tag is a small bit of action, a gesture, or figure of speech specific to one character. For example, you might have a character who rubs the side of his nose whenever he is really agitated, or a villain who sneers or snickers when he is about to strike. On the stage such tags are called "business." It is the "business" of identification. However, such minor tricks are not the only way to characterize; they should complement the way you reveal your characters through their actions and dialogue.

Plot lines and outlines

Plot is a vital element in a novel for young readers, especially in a realistic one in which there are no fantastic creatures to seduce the reader.

The plot—or story line—has sometimes been described as getting your character to the foot of the tree, getting him up the tree, and then figuring out how to get him down again. The length of time he is up in the tree, dangling his feet or falling from branch to branch like Pooh Bear on his disastrous honey-swiping trip, is a matter of style and diversion and secondary plot. But the main plot line should be a simple graph: to the tree, up the tree, down the tree.

Many writers find it necessary to outline a novel completely, writing a full paragraph or page for each chapter. These authors are unwilling to find themselves up the wrong tree or on the wrong branch at the wrong time. Others, however, find that a simpler outline suffices—a bare map with a word or two indicating the chapter elements. A few—like Newbery Award-winning author Sid Fleischman—use no plot outline at all. In Fleischman's words, "I like to wake each morning and find out what is going to happen next." However you decide to work, it is important that *you* be in control of the plot elements at all times. Like a juggler with several apples and oranges in the air, the author has to know just when to catch and just when to let go in order to keep the "act" moving smoothly.

Even writers who produce detailed or narrational outlines must realize that there are times when an outline has to be rewritten, as the story evolves into a novel. It is important to remember that *character is plot*, that the plot has to grow out of the characters, not be imposed upon them. Characters will often dictate new twists and turns to their authors.

Here are two examples: When I was first outlining (partial outline, not full) my YA historical novel *The Gift of Sarah Barker*, I planned that in the bittersweet and ironic ending, Sarah and Abel would be forced to leave the protected Shaker community where they had both grown up. They would get married; he would go off to fight in the Civil War on the North's side and be killed at Andersonville; and Sarah with the new baby in arms would return to New Vale, the community which had driven her out. However, as I got nearer to the end, my characters revolted. I was as much in love with Abel as Sarah was and could not possibly kill him off. And besides, I had made Sarah such a headstrong, powerful, loving, and nurturing young woman, I knew she would *never* have returned to the Shakers or give up her child. The ending was dictated by the characters. The plot flowed organically from them.

Another example comes from my novel *Sister Light, Sister Dark*, a high fantasy, sword-and-sorcery adventure. When I was jotting down my thoughts on the book, I planned to kill off Pynt, the chief secondary character, partially for pathos and partially because she was threatening to take over the novel and mostly (so I had convinced myself) so that I could be sure that my main character was totally alone. But when I got to the scene I had planned for

Pynt's demise, I simply could not write it. For several weeks I was stumped—entirely stopped in the book's forward progress, while I held long conversations with myself and my characters. Pynt simply would not die. At last I realized what was wrong: I was trying to have plot dictate to the characters. Instead, I wounded Pynt sorely and let my heroine Jenna move on without her. Finding her friend Pynt again became the climactic scene in the book and let Jenna make some strong emotional choices that would simply not have been possible if Pynt had conveniently died.

In other words, as the author, you need to listen to your characters. If you suddenly find yourself running behind, desparately trying to catch up, instead of being the leader of a band, put aside the book and revise the outline!

Discovering your style

In most novels (with the exception of fantasy and science fiction), style plays an understated role. Like type design, which has been called the invisible art, style in most novels works best when it is unobtrusive. One should, in author Gordon R. Dickson's phrase, "fall through the words into the story."

Still, the teenage book and the middle-grade novel demand to be written in the adolescent's own special language—slang or jargon. When that Pandora's box is opened, the problems that develop are legion.

Nothing dates as quickly as slang. Nothing dates a *relevant* book faster than out-of-date slang. Teenagers today would howl at the slang of teens fifteen years ago. When I was a teenager, in the fifties, we said "neat-o," "swinging," and "See you later, alligator." My own children, who were adolescents in the eighties, said "That's ex!" and "Take off!"

The following examples should prove this point. Here is a

paragraph from Betty Cavanna's *Going on Sixteen,* published in 1946:

> "I'm going to do my hair in a page boy," Anne was going on, and immediately Julie could see that half the other girls at the table considered the possibility of also doing their hair in page boys. "There's a picture in one of mother's magazines of the neatest way."

And then from *Academy Summer* by Nan Gilbert, published fifteen years later, in 1961:

> Ben missed the sarcasm. "It sure would be. Gosh, a kid fresh from junior high wouldn't have any incentive at all to go out for athletics."
> "It might very well give him a complex."
> "You said it. No, Monroe High's been pretty swell, but now it's time to move into a bigger world."

No self-respecting teenager talks that way today: *neat, gosh, swell.* These books are dated by their dialogue. They might as well be historical novels—except that they do not have the factual background that such novels require.

The trick is to have characters talk as children their same age would without resorting to slang. *Use words that soak up life,* indeed.

Underground and legitimate

Realistic novels deal with subjects that children today are intimately involved with; subjects they have whispered about surreptitiously or watched on the television when they were not supposed to; or wept about late in night in the comfort of their own beds.

In the past they appropriated adult books on such subjects, making them their own: *A Tale of Two Cities, A Catcher in the Rye.* Today they are sneaking Robert Ludlum and Stephen King.

Though writers should not shy away from strong material, it is just as important not to search out "hot" topics to write a book. The author's involvement in the subject or problem or theme of the novel should never overshadow the characters. You must communicate the emotional content without setting up a lecture with pat plots and flat characters who are simply mouthpieces. Novels that present the strong realities of our times in a fictional fashion are windows on the world to young readers. As writers we must explore—not simply write a story to exploit the latest phase, craze, or phrase.

Historical novels

The historical novel for young readers—both middle grades and young adults—is currently making a strong comeback. Especially when it can be tied easily to a school curriculum, the historical novel is popular with teachers and librarians as an easily swallowed history lesson for young readers.

Sir Walter Scott once said that a historical novel is any book about events at least sixty years ago. But for children, a historical novel is about anything that happened before they were born. That makes World War II ancient history, and the Korean War and Vietnam the Middle Ages. To a young reader, anything set fifteen years ago is historical. They ask their parents, "Was television invented when you were a child? Were planes? Were cars?"

But one should not forget the school curriculum. That is why there are so many Revolutionary War novels (from Esther Forbes's *Johnny Tremain* to James and Christopher Collier's *My Brother Sam is Dead*); Indian War novels (Scott O'Dell's *Island of the Blue Dolphins* to Conrad Richter's *The Light in the Forest*); Civil War novels (Paula Fox's *The Slave Dancer* to Belinda Hurmence's *A*

Girl Called Boy); World War II novels (Johanna Reiss' *The Upstairs Room* to my *The Devil's Arithmetic*); the Westward Movement (Patricia MacLachlan's *Sarah, Plain and Tall* to Ann Turner's *Third Girl from the Left*). They fit easily into an elementary or high school course. But for those fine novels about odd periods in history—the Bronze Age, for example, or India in the Raj period or Carolingian France—the marketplace sometimes asserts itself over literature. Two of the finest historical novels for young readers of the past twenty-five years disappeared because of their subject matter; A. Linevski's *An Old Tale Carved Out of Stone*, about early man on the cusp of change, and Martha Bennett Stiles' *A Star in the Forest*, a love story set in medieval France.

There are basically two kinds of historical novels: the *straight historical novel* and the *period novel*.

In the straight historical novel, the writer deals with events that have actually happened and people who actually lived, though placing them in a fictional context. There may be some invented characters for viewpoint; there may be interpolated or wholly made-up dialogue; there may be invented or guessed-at motivations. But the basic history and characters are real. Good examples of this are Rosemary Sutcliffe's moving *Song of the Dark Queen*, based on the life of Britain's Queen Boadicea; *Letters to Horseface* by F.N. Monjo, a charming recreation of a concert tour taken by the young Mozart; and Elaine Konigsburg's startling *The Second Mrs. Giaconda*, about Leonardo Da Vinci and his incorrigible apprentice, the street urchin Salai.

In the period novel, the people and events are made up, but the place and time exactly correspond to an era. In other words the setting is real, the broad history is correct, but what happens—and who it happens to—is made up. My *The Gift of Sarah Barker* is an example. So, too, Patricia

MacLachlan's *Sarah, Plain and Tall* and Paula Fox's *The Slave Dancer.* The characters are all originals, the landscapes realistic (though not actual), and the period touches authentic.

The greatest problem that faces writers of historical novels, though, is that attitudes as well as costumes and customs have changed. A child reader, so unforgiving, does not understand why—for example—anyone could justify slavery and believe black people were only partly human. Nor can they understand why parents would let their children go off on a long and dangerous trip across the Alps with no protection, as in the Children's Crusade. Or how the Jews could have been led, unprotesting, into the death camps.

A third kind of historical novel—the time travel novel—solves this problem by making history an experiential act. In the time travel novel, a young person of today ventures back into history with all his or her modern prejudices and modern attitudes intact. *That* child asks questions that a period child would not. The young black child in Belinda Hurmence's *A Girl Called Boy*, the Dutch teenager in Thea Beckman's *Crusade in Jeans*, and my Hannah/Chaya in *The Devil's Arithmetic* all become the reader's alter ego. It does not take less historical research on the part of an author, but it does solve that particular thorny problem of explaining attitudes.

In any novel using history as its base, the authenticity of the setting—the period landscape—must never be in doubt. When C.S. Forester praises the novel's "specificity," that must go double for the author writing in history. Sights, sounds, even smells must be evoked, within the forward movement of the story.

This passage from Mollie Hunter's *The Stronghold*, set in

Druidic Scotland during the days of the Roman raids, is masterful:

> In a flurry of sand and pebbles spurting from under his feet, he covered the part of the beach that lay between himself and the fire pit. The fire was lit there—it was always kept burning and needed only to be blown furiously into flaring life. The stack of dry peat to feed the blaze was ready beside it, and sheltered under the same covering of skins were the fire spears with their shafts dipped in seal oil and their heads bound with dried peat fibers.

Another example, this from Ann Turner's *The Way Home*, set in England in the Middle Ages, a powerful evocation:

> When she thought back later, after all had happened, Anne saw the village of Foxleigh on that last safe day of the spring of 1349 as if it were a painting, fixed forever on the wall of a church. The brown rutted road looped through crowded cottages so close Gilly could spit from her front step and hit Tom's door. The walls were gray and stained and the roof thatch let the rain in. Chickens pecked in the road next to bare-bottomed children playing with sticks and dollies. The alewife's house was in the middle of the village. Inside, at night, men sat and drank until their mouths dropped opened.

And from my *Children of the Wolf,* a story set in India in the 1920s in an orphanage by the side of the great sal forest:

> So thick with sal trees was this particular part of the jungle that it was shady even during the day. The sun might be overhead, but we were rarely able to see it through the green filtered light, until a single ray of sunshine would suddenly come through a rip in the fabric of leaves, reminding us there was another world beyond and above the jungle. Dark as it was, it was not altogether gloomy, for the air was filled with

the cries of rhesus monkeys and the steady *racheta-racheta* of the empty kerosene can fixed under the cart, with a protruding stick hitting against the wheels.

Another special problem of the historical novel is that of authentic dialogue. Sometimes anachronisms slip in—a cliché from the wrong era. (In a historical picture book set in Holland in the 1600s I wanted to say that a merman sounded like a foghorn, but my *Oxford English Dictionary* recorded no usage of the word foghorn until the 1700s. I found a different metaphor.) Sometimes a word whose reference has changed drastically can no longer be used. ("They threw the faggots on the fire" simply meant throwing logs on the fire. If you are writing a medieval historical novel, you will probably have to do without *that* particular word.) But more important, it is not possible to write in the exact argot of an early time.

There is really no way of knowing how people of a period in history spoke, and no one, especially not a young reader, would understand it. You must approximate speech patterns. A good trick is to write in formal English with no contractions.

"I am sorry, Ma'am, but I could not make it to the ball." Certainly that sounds more old fashioned than: "Sorry, babe, but I couldn't get to the dance."

Finally, if you want to write a historical or period novel, you *must* be true to the time. As John Stewig, in his excellent volume *Children and Literature*, writes:

> We all live within societal constraints though in our age these may seem to be rapidly disappearing. Even in our permissive era, some actions are possible or impossible, depending on the circumstances. So it was in any historic time.

Readers with twentieth century sensibilities may wish a story ended differently, but another ending may indeed not have been possible in another era. How did the character solve the problem, and how authentic was the solution in the context of the time?

Truth is a matter of the imagination.
                                   —Ursula K. Le Guin

‖ 8

Tripping the (Faster Than) Light Fantastic

JUST AS POETRY expresses a unique way of seeing the world, so does that most poetic of books, the fantasy or science fiction novel. Fantasy and poetry are natural for children. The world itself is new to them. A literature that celebrates newness—whether the newness of the future or the newness of the imagined—is as natural to the child reader as the world itself.

Many authors, critics, pedagogues have tried to define *fantasy literature*. In the classic essay "On Fairy Stories," J.R.R. Tolkien called it the subcreative art, that is a creation of a secondary world in which things happen "with arresting strangeness." On the other hand, May Hill Arbuthnot in *Children and Books* called a fantasy story "a tale of magic, often beginning realistically but merging quickly into adventures strange, astonishing, and dreamlike."

But perhaps a better definition might come from the

world of science fiction which now encompasses so many subgenres (many involving no science at all) that such writing is often called *speculative fiction*.

Speculative fiction is an excellent shorthand definition for fantasy literature in general, since it is a fiction that speculates on the limitless possibilities that this and other worlds hold. As the famous mathematician and biologist J.B.S. Haldane once said, "How do you know that the planet Mars isn't carried around by an angel?" We don't know—not really. It is up to the author of speculative fiction to give us windows that open onto all those possible worlds—with or without angels.

The breadth of fantasy literature is fantastic itself. It has touched on talking animals like Richard Adams' rabbits in *Watership Down;* talking inanimate objects like Thomas Disch's *The Brave Little Toaster;* time travel to an imagined past like Mark Twain's *A Connecticut Yankee in King Arthur's Court;* time travel to a real past like Belinda Hurmence's *A Girl Called Boy;* time travel to the future like Madeleine L'Engle's *A Wrinkle in Time.* It has touched ghost stories, monster stories, vampire stories, stories about dwarves, elves, dragons, wizards, spaceships—and far distant stars.

In order to make some sense of the great variety, I have divided the possible fantasy worlds into three categories: *Earthbound, Faerie,* and *Tourist.*

Created worlds

Earthbound fantasies are stories in which the action takes place in a world in which we live, though some of the characters may be fantastical. Examples of this kind of story are *The Wind in the Willows* (Kenneth Grahame), *James and the Giant Peach* (Roald Dahl), *Mistress Masham's Repose* (T.H. White), *The Borrowers* (Mary Norton), *Charlotte's Web* (E.B. White), and *Mary Poppins* (P.L. Travers). These earths are full of wonders we will never meet outside the pages of a book: friendships between rats and moles who wear smoking jackets; a boy's visit with talking bugs; the leftover Lilliputians who live in a gazebo; the tiny behind-the-walls world of little people who live by borrowing things from humans; a spider who spins messages in her web to save her best friend, a pig; a miracle-making British nanny. These are books that fulfill Tolkien's request that fantasy be founded "on a recognition of fact but not a slavery to it."

The second category, *Faerie*, is named after that mythic land where the fairy creatures dwell. In faerie books, the action takes place in a world totally apart from ours, impinging on Earth in neither time nor space. Outstanding examples of *Faerie* books are Tolkien's *The Hobbit* and *Lord of the Rings*, Ursula K. Le Guin's *The Wizard of Earthsea*, Patricia McKillip's *The Riddle-Master of Hed*.

Finally, there are *Tourist* fantasies, in which a traveler from Earth finds his way to another world or into another time and adventures there. *Alice's Adventures in Wonderland* is an obvious example. In C.S. Lewis' first Narnia book, *The Lion, the Witch and the Wardrobe*, four children go through the wardrobe to another, magic-filled realm. A boy named Milo rides his toy car through Norton Juster's *The Phantom Tollbooth* and finds a strange world on the other side. Phillipa Pearce's young hero goes back and forth in time in *Tom's Midnight Garden*. And my young Jewish heroine Hannah finds herself thrown back into the time of the Holocaust when she opens the door for Elijah at a family seder in modern New York City in *The Devil's Arithmetic*.

The word is belief

Kenneth Grahame, author of *The Wind in the Willows*, once wrote about the kind of belief that an author and reader both must bring to fantasy novels: "Whatever its components, truth is not necessarily one of them. A dragon, for instance, is a more enduring animal than a pterodactyl. I have never yet met anyone who really believed in a pterodactyl, but every honest person believes in dragons—down in the back-kitchen of his consciousness."

Belief is the key to making fantasy fiction live.

Not only must the reader believe in the fantasy while reading it, the author must believe in it while writing it. If the author is skeptical of his own creation, it will translate easily into condescension: "I, of course, don't believe a word of this stuff, but you—dear kiddies—will gobble it up."

There are ways to help along this authorial belief:

- Make up geneological charts. Tolkien did so for *The Lord of the Rings*. Knowing as much as you can about the backgrounds of your fantastic characters will make them more real.

- Draw detailed maps of the world. Does your main city lie north or east of the deep dark woods? Will they be turning left or right out of the castle gates? One way to keep track of quests is to actually chart the area as L. Frank Baum did for the Oz books.

- Make up a Bible for your world, with major proverbs or wise adages listed. I did this for *Sister Light, Sister Dark*.

In other words, surrender yourself to your own fantasy world for the time you are writing it. After all, isn't *surrender* what you ask of your readers? More than Coleridge's lukewarm dictum about "the willing suspension of disbelief," you need readers who will give themselves up completely.

As George MacDonald wrote in his classic fantasy tale, *The Golden Key:*

> The Old Man of the Earth stooped over the floor of the cave, raised a huge stone from it, and left it leaning. It disclosed a great hole that went plumb down.
>
> "That is the way," he said.
>
> "But there are no stairs."
>
> "You must throw yourself in. There is no other way."

The author asks that of the reader: to throw himself into the fantasy because there is really no other way.

The laws of fantasy

A boy wrote to me recently about my fantasy novel *Dragon's Blood:* "I read the book thirteen times. There are some days when I wake up and I think I really *am* Jakkin Stewart."

The only way such belief on a reader's part can be gained is by the author's own belief and fair play. By that I mean that *logic* must be the most important element in a fantasy book.

Logic? But isn't fantasy based on an illogical premise? Look at some of the premises of fantasy novels: a toy Indian in a cupboard can come alive, a spider can spin advertising slogans in her web to help save a pig from being turned into bacon, a little girl can adventure with a pack of cards. Those are all illogical by the logic we know. But once you set up any of these premises as the basis of a novel, everything after that must flow logically. As novelist Lloyd Alexander writes, "The Muse in charge of Fantasy wears good sensible shoes."

The created fantasy world must have its own immutable laws. Once those laws have been established, they cannot be set aside at the author's whim for the demands of plot.

The tools needed to make the unreal real, to make the fantasy world actual and factual, are three: *place, character, style.*

First, place. The piling up of corroborating details that help inspire the reader's belief creates the place. If you read any of the fantasy novels I have mentioned, you will see that the authors have such a visual sense of their fantasy world, it is impossible not to see it through their eyes. Author-critic Eleanor Cameron calls it "the compelling power of place."

This is from *Alice in Wonderland* as Alice is falling down the rabbit hole:

> Either the well was very deep, or she fell very slowly, for she had plenty of time as she went down to look about her, and to wonder what was going to happen next. First, she tried to look down and make out what she was coming to, but it was too dark to see anything: then she looked at the sides of the well, and noticed that they were filled with cupboards and book-shelves; here and there she saw maps and pictures hung upon pegs. She took down a jar from one of the shelves as she passed: it was labeled ORANGE MARMALADE, but to her great disappointment it was empty: she did not like to drop the jar, for fear of killing somebody underneath, so managed to put it into one of the cupboards as she fell past it.

And this is from the first of the Narnia books, *The Lion, the Witch and the Wardrobe*, as young Lucy comes to tea with Mr. Tumnus the faun:

> Lucy thought she had never been in a nicer place. It was a little, dry, clean cave of reddish stone with a carpet on the floor and two little chairs ("one for me and one for a friend," said Mr.

Tumnus) and a table and a dresser and a mantelpiece over the fire and above that a picture of an old Faun with a grey beard. In one corner there was a door which Lucy thought must lead to Mr. Tumnus' bedroom, and on one wall was a shelf full of books. Lucy looked at these while he was setting out the tea things. They had titles like *The Life and Letters of Silenus* or *Nymphs and Their Ways* or *Men, Monks and Gamekeepers: A Study in Popular Legend* or *Is Man a Myth?*

And this last is a description of the wizard's warren under the fountain, from my book *The Wizard of Washington Square*.

> The Wizard sat in a large velvet-cushioned oak chair in front of a tremendous table. The table was as long as a large door and had nine sturdy legs, each ending in a claw. One claw clutched a wooden ball and, at odd moments, it would suddenly roll the ball to another leg. Then that claw would snatch the ball and stand very proudly on it. In this way, every few minutes the table would take on a slightly different tilt. Each time the game began again, all the beakers and bowls and pitchers and jars on top of the table—for the table was littered with glassware and crockery—would jangle and clank. But surprisingly, nothing was ever broken.

The details of place are precise: the jar of marmalade in the long, dark tunnel cupboard; the book titles on the genteel faun's bookshelf; the crockery set a-rattling on the table's surface. Nothing is fuzzy or half-visualized. In fact, the reader believes that the authors have been to these places and are reporting what they have seen.

If, as Henry James has said about the novel, its supreme virtue is its "solidity of specificiation," it is twice as true about any work of fantasy. In every work of realistic fiction, certain descriptions are givens. Write down "an apartment house" or "a ranch house" or "meadow," and the reader has an immediate visual response. But if the writer says "tunnel cupboard" or "faun's parlor" or "wizard's warren" without specific details, the reader does not have a visual image of these places. And it all has to be done solidly. As Lloyd Alexander has written about his own fantasy series, the Prydain books, "What appears gossamer is underneath solid as prestressed concrete."

Along with making genealogical charts, consulting maps, studying the Bible to help create the necessary believability, the writer might try one of these:

- Create a travelogue, taking yourself on trips to points of special interest, making up the guide's spiel.

- Write an encyclopedia article that includes customs, laws, historical background, or the flora and fauna of the land you have created. Detail the Gross National Product. I did this for the information about Austar IV in my *Pit Dragon* trilogy and it worked so well, I used some of it as an encyclopedia extract at the beginning of each book.

- Build a diorama room or rooms in which your fictional people will be living, adding dimension to your descriptions.

Even if you never use half the material you have gathered or built, it will help you reconstruct the place for the reader. What you don't put down can be as important as what you do.

Character

Just as carefully, the fantasist has to build up character, remembering, of course, that characters are better built by their actions and reactions than endless descriptions. The dictum, as in any novel, is SHOW DON'T TELL.

However, where a realistic novelist might get away with

quick flash of the features of a major player, the fantasy writer must present careful close-ups. After all, these characters may have some interesting quirks besides their personality quirks. Not many of us have met an E. Nesbit Psammead or a Tolkien Hobbit on our daily rounds, nor could we summon one up in the mind's eye without having read the books. And even if we have seen a lion or an English nanny or a stuffed bear in reality, they are not anything like Mary Poppins or Winnie-the-Pooh. Once you have met them, the actual is transformed into the magical.

Readers, too, are transformed by the meeting.

The magic that works the transformation is again the magic of detail. The piling up of visual attributes along with the physical and emotional action/reaction, in the end utterly convinces the reader that the unreal *is* real. Often some homey detail is what does it. For example, once you know that the psammead suffers horribly if he gets wet or that hobbits spin long and unbroken tales about their family trees and have hair on *top* of their feet, you absolutely *know* they exist.

It is just as important to spell out the horrors. The wicked villains need to be as vivid as the hero, or else the hero is left with only a cardboard cutout to fight (and conquer). Wicked figures should not be shrugged off with a wimpy adjective or adverb, as in so many of the Victorian horror stories: "It was the ineffable," or "It was the unknowable," or "It was the unutterable." Modern young readers do not suffer from Victorian sensibilities where horror is concerned. They have watched "Friday the 13th, Part 27" and giggled. The best fantasy and science fiction tales make the Bad Guys "utterable" and "knowable" and "effable," categorizing the horrors with as much detail as the author dare muster. Or can stomach.

Yet black and white, good against evil, is no longer acceptable in fantasy and science fiction novels. Even the villains have to have motivation and reasons for villainy. They may not be the hero's reasons, but they must be logical within the context of the story, the realm, and the telling.

The voices of fantasy

What is unique to fantasy is the role played by style or voice.

There is nothing tame in the great fantasy novels. Tendrils of green lianas crawl across the paths. Strange, invisible beasts call from behind midnight trees. The world is moonlit, a chiaroscuro land where light and dark are in constant shadow play. The voice we tell these stories in must reflect those worlds.

Of the many possible voices of fantasy, here are three of the most popular: *the oracle, the schoolboy's,* and *the fool's.*

The oracular voice speaks in the poetic, metaphoric mode, from hollow caves, out of swirling mists. And it often speaks in riddles, singing with bardic full-chest tones. This is the sound of high fantasy, where epic battles rage across the pages of the book. Tolkien, Le Guin, McKillip are all masters of this particular voice. And it is no coincidence that actual riddles play an important role in their books. As the young apprentice Ged in Le Guin's *The Wizard of Earthsea* is told by his master:

> This sorcery is not a game we play for pleasure or for praise. Think of this: that every word, every act of our Art is said and is done for good or for evil. Before you speak or do you must know the price that is to pay.

He is being told, poetically, that stricture inherent in all the oracular fantasies: *magic has consequences.*

The oracular tones are the full *basso profundo* of fantasy

dialects, the ground bass on which melodies of the others overswell. The words are sometimes archaic, fanciful, Latinate, sonorous. There is frequent use of alliterations. The sentences, like chants, often end in a full stop, the strong stress syllable that reminds the reader of a knell rung on a full set of bells. One can actually declaim high fantasy, singing out whole paragraphs, even chapters. If it were set to music, it would be Beethoven, full and echoing, resonant, touching deep into the most private places of the heart.

The schoolboy voice is more securely set in the here-and-now. While fantasy figures bend and bow around it, the voice remains childlike, innocent, a sensible commentary on the imaginary. Writers like E. Nesbit, C. S. Lewis, Natalie Babbitt, and Diana Wynne Jones use this voice remarkably well. The schoolboy voice speaks in ordinary tones about the extraordinary, recalling us to our humanity in the midst of the fantastic.

A Nesbit child, reacting to her first meeting with a psammead, that extraordinary tubby-bodied, spider-shaped creature with hands and feet like a monkey's and eyes on long horns, says: "What on earth is it? . . . Shall we take it home?"

And C. S. Lewis' British schoolboy Eustace, facing the elegant talking mouse Reepicheep, who has just bowed and kissed Lucy's hand, remonstrates, "Ugh, take it away. . . . I hate mice. And I never could bear performing animals. They're silly and vulgar and—sentimental."

Two very real schoolchildren's reactions to marvels: opposite, apposite, and very true to form.

And when Winnie Foster, in Babbitt's *Tuck Everlasting*, hears the strange story of the Tucks and their water of everlasting life, she does not think about the unbelievability of their history. Rather she zeroes in on the humanity confronting her, thinking:

> It was the strangest story Winnie had ever heard. She soon suspected they have never told it before, except to each other—that she was their first real audience; for they gathered around her like children at their mother's knee, each trying to claim her attention, and sometimes they talked at once, and interrupted each other in their eagerness.

There is the key to the schoolboy voice. The child in this kind of fantasy takes over the role of the adult, shepherding the fantastic creatures through their magical paces; guiding and guarding them—even when terribly frightened—for this world belongs to the child, this world into which magic has slipped. It is not the fact of the magic that is startling, because children expect that kind of magic to occur, but rather it is the vulnerability of the creatures of magic, a bit sad in their magnificence, sometimes "silly and vulgar and—sentimental."

These are the middle tones, as plain yet fantastic as a Bach fugue; a simple tune made more complex by interweaving with the magic. It is everyday language set against a backdrop of the extraordinary.

The third voice, *the fool's*, is high and piercing, full of ridiculous trills and anachronisms, word plays and puns. Yet underneath the pratfalls and the bulbous-nose mask, behind the wild shrieks of laughter and the shaking of the metaphoric slapsticks, lie deep serious thoughts.

Writers like Lewis Carroll, Sid Fleischman, and Norton Juster are masters at this voice. There is meaning and significance hidden amid the silliness, as in this quote from Carroll:

". . . you should say what you mean," the March Hare went on.

"I do," Alice hastily replied, "at least—at least I mean what I say—that's the same thing, you know."

"Not the same a bit!" said the Hatter. "Why, you might just as well say 'I see what I eat' is the same thing as 'I eat what I see'!"

"You might just as well say," added the March Hare, "that 'I like what I get' is the same thing as 'I get what I like'!"

"You might just as well say," added the Dormouse, which seemed to be talking in its sleep, "that 'I breathe when I sleep' is the same thing as 'I sleep when I breathe'!"

"It *is* the same thing with you," said the Hatter.

That is not just straight silliness. It is so applicable to everyday life that at the time of the Watergate hearings the *Alice* books were quoted practically every day by newspaper and TV commentators.

What makes this kind of voice work is hyperbole—the mad exaggeration for effect—like Fleischman's Chancy in *Chancy and the Grand Rascal*, who is so skinny he'd "have to stand twice to throw a shadow." And word games as in Juster's *Phantom Tollbooth:*

"If you please," said Milo. . . . "your palace is beautiful."

"Exquisite," corrected the duke.

"Lovely," counseled the minister.

"Handsome," recommended the count.

"Pretty," hinted the earl.

"Charming," submitted the undersecretary.

"*SILENCE*," suggested the king.

Science fiction has its special voices, too, such as the *anchorman*, which is a straightforward documentary style that gives names, dates, places, inventions, cogwheels, initials, data where the science "stuff" is more interestingly and lovingly presented than the characterizations. Or the

doomsayer voice which, like the fantasy *oracular* voice uses
extensive metaphors and is deeply resonant. But the subject matter is the end of the world—or the beginning; and
artifacts alternate with poetry. There is also the *All-Amer-
ica Boy* voice, a kind of comic break "gee whiz" style. This
is white bread in outer space; science and fiction where the
rocketship has training wheels, and the pilot never curses.

The style or voice is a signal to the reader. It puts the
mood of the piece into place even before the action begins.
Nowhere is attention to style more important than in the
genre of the fantastic. In realistic writing, style tends to be
invisible. In realistic writing, style tends to be invisible. In
fantasy and science fiction novels, the voice is important for
creating texture, character, believability.

Vision

It is not only in style that fantasy differs from realistic
fiction. Vision (also known as *theme* or *subtext*) also plays a
key role. This is the novel in which the epic sweep, the
chance to play out large gestures, the battles of good vs.
evil rage across the page.

While realistic fiction deals with small everyday truths,
fantasy, by its very remove from reality, can deal with
Truth with a capital T. Realistic fiction shows us so well the
tiny evasions and lies we indulge in daily. Fantasy shows us
the Great Lie.

Alfred North Whitehead wrote: "Literature exists only
to express and develop that imaginative world which is our
life, the kingdom which is within us." Fantasy shows the
reader the widest borders of that kingdom and sounds the
depths of that world.

It is just such imaginative probing that makes some
adults mistrust fantasy. Even today, we hear the argument
that books of fantasy wean the child from the real world,

giving him no hold on reality. However, these books speak to the unconscious in the reader, opening and widening the areas of experience. They hone an aesthetic appreciation in the reading child, teaching him about things that can be found in that realm of wonder—the imagination. The fantasy novel also instills values, for these are the books that dare use the words that have become the pornography of innocence: words like *truth, honor, love, hate, courage, evil* and *good*. They do it not by setting down a moral, but by telling a story.

As the Master Hand in *The Wizard of Earthsea* tells young Ged: "To light a candle is to cast a shadow." The writer lights many candles in a good fantasy novel. The shadows they cast in a child's soul will last for the rest of his life.

*The need to know surely and accurately is
a basic hunger. . . .*
                                    —May Hill Arbuthnot

‖ 9

Nonfiction Books

"**N**OW WHAT I WANT is facts. Teach these boys and girls nothing but facts. Facts alone are wanted in life. Plant nothing else and root out everything else. You can form the minds of reasoning animals only upon facts. Nothing else will ever be of any service to them."

Does that sound like your ninth-grade teacher? Or a local librarian? Or the principal of your child's elementary school? It is actually Mr. Gradgrind in Dickens' *Hard Times.* Yet over a hundred years later, there are still those who echo the sentiments of the unsentimental, unimaginative Mr. G.

I even met an eight-year-old boy who sounded like him. He cornered me one day after having dismissed my gift of a fantasy book with a contemptuous sniff.

"You know what boys my age like?" he inquired rhetorically. "They like *real* books. They like the facts."

To my eight-year-old friend, *real* was equivalent to *facts.*

He was mistaking raw facts for information. And it is information, not just raw facts, that most children want.

Information or facts

It is important to draw that distinction immediately when talking about nonfiction: facts, or data, *vs.* information, or what the data says.

For example, if a boatman stands at the bow and shouts: "Mark twelve, mark ten, mark six, mark four, mark twain," he is giving data to the helmsman. But the helmsman is receiving the following information: "The water is getting awfully shallow. Do something, quick."

An untrained ear would not hear it as information, only as facts.

It is the nonfiction writer's problem to turn that data into information. Data is useful only to the trained ear and eye. As information, it speaks to anyone who takes the time to listen. Information is useful, it is palatable, it is fascinating. And it is compelling to the reader.

Changing data into information is a creative process. It is the first of a series of processes that make the writing of nonfiction as creative as the writing of fiction.

Changing data into information consists of organizing, distilling, and processing. It consists of making comparisons and finding commonalities. All these things can be summed up in one word: *recognition.*

For example, for a book I wrote about the history and lore of kite flying, *World on a String,* first I collected an assortment of *facts:* kites originated almost 3000 years ago in China; religious kite flying is done in Japan; intricate centipede and dragon kites abound in Korea; weather kites were important in America; Marconi used a kite antenna for his wireless experiments; Benjamin Franklin flew a kite in a thunderstorm and proved the sky was full of electricity.

Lots of *data*. Then I began to see a common thread, a *theme*—kites rose in the East and flowered there in beauty and serenity. When they traveled to the West, they became useful. And *that* is information. Once I had that, the book began to achieve a balance, a point of view, a style, and all because I had found a thread that could wind through the narrative of my kite history.

Or another example from my own writing: I was working on a biography of George Fox, the first Quaker. I gathered facts, data: Fox was arrested for refusing to sign an oath of loyalty to the king; he was put in jail for refusing to fight in the Commonwealth army; he was beaten by mobs for preaching that God lives in every man. Then I began to see that George Fox had a lot to say to the young people of the day. With his long hair and odd clothes, with his pronouncements in favor of women, against slavery, against war—even with his funny "thee's" and "thou's"—he had a spirit that matched any of the young radicals of our era. Again, information, then a thread that could run through the entire book.

What I achieved in those two books is what Arthur Koestler speaks of in *The Act of Creation*. He calls it "The sudden shaking together of two previously unconnected matrices." It is known as the Eureka Act in science. It is known as the *A-ha* in Gestalt Therapy. It is the light bulb above a person's head in the comic strips. It is *recognition*.

Significant research

Another creative part of nonfiction writing is the research for a book on a factual subject. Research *can* be only a collecting of data. It can be the journalist's who-what-when-where-how. But the truly creative researcher is the one who asks not only what happened, but *what does it mean?* Not only how did it happen, but *how does it affect other things?* In other words, the creative researcher is thinking of data raised to the plane of information. The creative researcher is actively seeking out ways of turning data—at the very moment of researching—into information. When you do this, you are going to find more data because you are going to be moving on several planes at once.

Creative research is made up of four parts: intuitive guesses, detective work, *chutzpah*, and just plain luck. The first three you can cultivate. The last, somehow, always follows after, like the tail on one of Bo-Peep's sheep.

The *intuitive guess* is the competent, educated guess that leads a researcher on to discovery. It is what Suzanne Langer meant when she wrote that "Most discoveries are suddenly seen things that were always there."

The *detective work* is the initial background stage, the finding of various sources. Any good library will have a detailed list of reference books in the *Guide to Reference Books*. Checking the *Reader's Guide to Periodical Literature* will tell you about magazine articles on your subject in over 150 different periodicals. *The American Library Directory* and the *Subject Collection: A Guide to Special Book Collections in Libraries* are also helpful. *Poole's Index to Periodical Literature* lists the contents of American and British magazines published between 1802 and 1906. *The New York Times Index* has bound volumes and a microfilm index that go back to 1851. And *The London Times Index* goes all the way back to 1790. *The Cumulative Book Index* lists books published since 1898. These help you to zero in on the available material. Once you have done the necessary detective work, you are ready to begin. And there are many other indexes to poetry, short stories, etc., that you will find in a good reference department of a public library.

Chutzpah, the Yiddish word for gall or guts, is what you need in tracking down another source of background material—individuals who can help you. Since researching in books alone often leaves you with a dry, stolid view of a subject, it helps to find someone experienced with your subject to give you a new current view. Contacting such a person—or persons—often takes courage, gall, *chutzpah*.

Just plain *luck* will follow.

Let me give you an example of how this four-part backgrounding works. When I was a child I devoured pirate books. I had a crush on Captain Kidd, Henry Morgan, and Blackbeard. In the course of my reading, I happened upon two women pirates—Anne Bonney and Mary Reade. Years later, thinking of a subject for a nonfiction book, I remembered these two "ladies."

It was then I made my *intuitive guess:* where there were two women pirates, there were probably more. I had heard of women like Deborah Sampson disguising themselves as men and joining the Revolutionary Army. Why not women doing the same aboard ship? Surely, I told myself, there were more than two female pirates. It turned out that I was correct.

Then began my detective work. One magazine I tracked down was a one-shot entitled *Treasure Hunters.* A minuscule biography of the author, Robert I. Nesmith, mentioned that he lived in Rye, New York. So I turned my *detective work* into *chutzpah.*

Rye, New York was one town away from my parents' home, so I called Mr. Nesmith and was ready to invite myself over to talk about pirates—and ladies—with him.

And that was when *luck* came in. Mr. Nesmith invited me over immediately. He turned out to have the world's largest collection of published and unpublished piratania. He was so delighted with my novel idea that he gave me free run of his library and helped me with my research. *Luck*, indeed. *Pirates in Petticoats* was published in 1963, and it is still the only book of its kind.

Notes and files

Some writers put their notes in little notebooks or large looseleafs; some on scraps of paper. I believe, however, that the best way is to use file cards, which can be easily arranged and rearranged as your book grows. They are also easy to carry into libraries.

Take care. Notes taken one, two, three months earlier in haste might as well have been taken by a Martian as yourself. Here is some necessary advice:

1. Write clearly and precisely in pen.

2. Put in quotes everything that comes directly from a source, and scribble "paraphrase" or "mine" next to anything that is your own interpretation.

3. Note on each card the name of the book, author, and the library where you found it. Otherwise, if you are using a number of different libraries, you can waste many precious hours trying to trace a book to check a quote if you do not remember where you found the book.

4. Check each book's bibliography and write *its* sources down. In that way, you enlarge the scope of your own research.

These may sound like simple-minded rules, but in the course of writing my nonfiction books, I have learned these things by experience.

Once you have amassed your data, thought about some connecting links, and made your initial *A-ha*'s, you are ready to write your nonfiction book.

The writing phase: outlines

Jean Karl, a former juvenile book editor, asks this question in her *From Childhood to Childhood*: ". . . how will authors demonstrate where facts imbedded in wisdom can lead? How can authors create books that will make children yearn for wisdom that lies beyond facts, without preaching, without pouring either the facts or the children into precast molds?"

Those are questions worth pondering. The problem is to put the meat (information) on the bones (data) without preaching. To teach without sounding as though you are teaching, reaching out not only for new subjects but for new approaches.

The new approach begins, of course, when you make your first *A-ha*. It continues through the next step—making an outline.

Outlines are an absolute necessity when writing nonfiction. An outline is like a road map. Whether the territory is previously explored or not, a road map will let you see at a glance the entire area to be traveled. It will also help you when the going gets rough. But just as road maps are updated whenever new roads have been added, so an outline has to change as your data and information grow. When the writer really gets into his information, when he experiences the Eureka phenomenon, it is inevitable (and exciting, too) that the outline will have to be changed.

The outline can serve another function, too. It is a selling tool. If your subject is strange enough, original enough, then you may be able to tease an editor into a contract with the outline alone (usually after you have some publication credits). The outline should not be of trivial matters, but detailed chapter-by-chapter plans of the books. In the case of my books, *Friend* and *The Wizard Islands*, the outline was also accompanied by prefatory material, author's notes, and forewords. Some of my outlines have been as long as twenty pages. In each instance, the final book was quite different from the original outline—better, I think, because I had additional information by the time I had finished.

An example of my own outline technique follows. It is from a twelve-page outline that I submitted for my biography *Friend: The Story of George Fox and the Quakers.*

GEORGE FOX AND THE INNER LIGHT
OUTLINE

Ch. I: The Righteous Christer
"If George says Verily, there is no altering him."
Birth and early life of George Fox, growing up in a poor but religious English home in the seventeenth century. Physical description and a character sketch of Fox. Also a sketch of the religious temper of the mid-seventeenth century that culminated in the great achievements of religious toleration and constitutional monarchy. It stemmed mainly from the upsurge of *personal* religion among the common people.

Ch. 2: The Man in Leather Breeches
"Here are my leather breeches which frighten all the priests and professors."
Early preaching and brutal jail experiences of Fox. His growth as a mystic, a proselytizer, and a strong man of religion who set himself up against the established churches with their priests and the wandering preachers of some 176 different sects. Fox's attack on organized religion, the priesthood, the churches as "houses" of god. His use of plain speech. His early convictions of the brotherhood of men, God in every man, and his jailings for these convictions.

I included a thumbnail sketch of Fox's life in two pages, five pages of chapter-by-chapter breakdown, and a five-page prologue that was eventually used, almost word-for-word, in the book. But the above two chapter descriptions became chapters 1–5 in the finished book, for as my knowledge of George Fox grew, so did the book. And what began as a projected ten-chapter biography ended up seventeen long chapters, plus a prologue and an epilogue, and an Author's Note to boot.

Good books grow. Good outlines allow such growth.

There are basically four kinds of nonfiction books for young readers: biography, history, science, and how-to. Occasionally they overlap one another. Each has problems peculiar to its genre, but they all have several things in common.

The primary danger facing anyone writing a nonfiction book for young readers is style. You must sail between the Scylla and Charybdis of jargon and cuteness.

On the one hand, there is the danger of falling back on the jargon of your subject. Especially in the sciences and social sciences this is true. But it also happens in how-to books. Aldous Huxley, in a brilliant though dense book, *Literature and Science*, roundly castigates the scientists for their self-imposed jabberwocky. He jibes: "A rose is a rose is a rose is RNA, DNA, polypeptide chares of amino acids. . . ." But at the same time he takes a swipe at the poets and "creative" writers who are afraid to tackle scientific subjects. Why shouldn't we have a Stephen Jay Gould's *The Flamingo's Smile* or a Carl Sagan's *The Dragons of Eden* for budding young scientists?

If jargon is the danger on the one hand, an equal danger is coyness. Many writers affect it when writing for young people. It is the little-books-for-little-minds syndrome. However, it is possible to write creative nonfiction without falling back into soppy story lines or the dear-reader's style that is so condescending.

In a *New York Times Book Review* article, Eve Merriam

satirized this horrible tendency with a piece entitled "The Poolitzer Prizes." She made up titles like *Let's Find Out about Doughnut Holes, Hortense the Happy Hypotenuse* and *Our Friend the Battery Cell.* The problem with these titles is that they are perilously close to titles editors reject—or publish—daily.

Making data come alive

A startling story line is not necessary in order to capture a child's interest in a nonfiction idea. But something *is* needed to make the data come alive to a child reader. Since facts alone cannot give the young reader an adequate handle on a factual subject, the writer must supply a substitute handle. Again, that is where the creative part of creative nonfiction comes in.

At the end of any book of nonfiction, for whatever age group it is intended, you should append two things—an index and a bibliography. It will be up to the editor to decide if the book actually needs a very detailed bibliography. Perhaps a simple "Recommended for Further Reading" list will do. However, you should send it along for two reasons: It authenticates your material, and it gives the copy editor a leg up on checking and rechecking your facts and quotes. Every author, even the best and most precise scholar, makes an occasional mistake in copying or typing. That is one of the reasons a publishing house has a copy editor—to catch any little mistake. The index cannot, of course, be handled until the book is in page proofs, since page references are needed. Often the publisher will hire a professional indexer to make your index for you, but many authors prefer to do their own.

Biography

Elizabeth Gray Vining, a noted author, wrote that one day the figure of William Penn came up and tapped her on the shoulder. After that, she had to write his biography.

All biographies should be written that way—when a historical personage taps you on the shoulder. You do not have to love or admire the person. You do not even have to like him. But you need to empathize with your subject. And when you are tapped on the shoulder, you should respond.

Such a commitment does not preclude objectivity. Indeed, especially in biography, the writer must be prepared to see the other side of the historical coin. A biographer must not sell his soul, as one wit put it, "for a pot of message."

The biographer has to be able to be both committed and objective. There is not one saint or sinner whose life story would not be more readable, more recognizable, more affecting if the objective truths were sifted from the subjective myths. As George Sims wrote cynically, "All biographies should have the subtitle: myth versus reality." Keep his suggestion in mind as you write, so that you will *not* have to append such a subtitle.

Especially in writing about the lives of saints, one has to walk carefully between worship and cynical disdain, between hagiography and "debunkum." Nothing is duller to the reader than a series of incidents in the life of a totally virtuous man or woman. But if you scratch the surface of most of the so-called totally virtuous saints, you will find them human. It is their very humanity rather than their godliness that makes them so fascinating. St. Paul without sin—uninteresting. Preacher John Donne without the libertine John—unthinkable. Ghandi without his early marriage problems—dehumanized. What makes these people "saints" is the fact that they rose above their human problems. What makes others "sinners" is that they sank under the weight.

To write *any* biography one must balance both positions: sinner and saint. How to find the man or woman behind the mask of history is the problem. That is the challenge, of course, cutting through history's tidyings-up, sorting through the legends that all powerful persons leave in their wakes.

It is important in writing biographies to get to the source. The scholars call the material that issued either directly from the mouth or pen of the subject or from contemporaries *primary sources. Secondary sources* are all that has been written since.

Some wonderful biographies written recently for young readers that should not be missed are Russell Freedman's *Lincoln: A Photobiography;* Rhoda Blumberg's *Commodore Perry in the Land of the Shōgun;* Kathleen Kudlinski's *Rachel Carson: Pioneer of Ecology;* Jean Fritz's *The Double Life of Pocahontas;* and interestingly, a pop-up book, *Leonardo Da Vinci* by Alice and Martin Provensen.

Quotations

Which brings us to the biggest technical problem in writing biography: to quote or not to quote.

There are two schools of thought on the problem of quotations. The first holds that you can put into quotes only what has been documented, either in direct speech or conversations reported by friends, letters from the subject or journals. André Maurois outlined this orthodox view succinctly: "Under no account has the biographer a right to invent a single fact. . . . He should not put into his hero's mouth nor attribute to any character, sentences they have not spoken." I would add to that, *or written.*

The second school holds that you can make an approximation of what the subject probably would have said in such circumstances, using things the subject has said or written in similar situations or simply making an educated guess based on thorough period research. Margery Fisher explained this view in her excellent book, *Matters of Fact* (regrettably out of print, but possibly available in a public library): "To draw a line too sharply between known fact and reasonable deduction would be to deny [children] a great deal of persuasive detail."

In my writing, I take the more orthodox approach, though my first book, *Pirates in Petticoats*, is replete with imagined conversations. I now feel that, if you are writing biography, what you quote from your subject must be documentable. Interpolated conversations belong to historical fiction. If you write such a book, be sure that words to the effect that "A novel based on the life of _____" are under your title.

The main problem facing a biographer is that he must make sense out of a subject, he must go beyond actions to interpret character. In fact, there must be a good deal of the lay psychologist and the novelist in every biographer. To quote Margery Fisher again: "Biography is an illusion, a fiction in the guise of fact." It is an especially exciting kind of book to write—precisely because of these problems.

History

When writing a book about history, it is important to remember that no historical period or historical event exists in a vacuum. Once not so long ago—about thirty years to be exact—history in the schools was taught as a succession of certain names, dates, places. I know, for I was taught that way. But today, the emphasis is on *understanding* what led to those certain names, dates, places.

So the writer of nonfiction books of history must guide the young reader into making the connections between past and present, or between the past and present of that book. The emphasis is on that word "guide." For children are not "small vessels crying to be filled with the word of truth, but rational individuals who can think for themselves," as author-editor Jean Karl wrote.

The research for a historical book may lead you into many unsuspected backwaters. Looking up my material for *Friend* introduced me to several characters I would love to put into a novel, incidents that could climax a stirring historical tale, even phrases that suggest a picture book. Nothing is lost in your research. It just gets stored in your files or your memory for further use.

The author of a nonfiction book must remember this simple rule: A steady development of events or facts makes for a steady reader. If you allow yourself many digressions or detours or irrelevancies, your book will be too complex for even the most sophisticated reader. Like a good mystery book, the good historical nonfiction book unfolds its clues.

Some excellent historical books to use as examples are: *To Be a Slave* by Julius B. Lester; *Chimney Sweeps* by James Cross Giblin; *Cathedral* by David Macaulay; *Strange Footprints on the Land* by Constance Irwin; *The Luttrell Village* by Sheila Sancha; and anything by Milton Meltzer.

Science

Popular science for children is fast becoming a new art form. In it, the writer must blend the textbook with reportage, the philosophical essay and a sociological forecast, to paraphrase Huxley.

Unfortunately, there has grown up in the years since science has taken its benevolent toll on man, a feeling that fact and fancy should not mix. Keats damned the man who explained the rainbow, saying he had robbed it of its poetry. Yet, it need not be so. Science fiction is one voice crying this out. And good science writing for children is another.

There are three interesting, poetic, yet scientifically correct methods of blending science and poetry in a book for young readers, three "tricks of the trade." They are the use of nonverbal or experimental examples, metaphor, and aphorism.

Nonverbal or experimental examples are pictures or experiments that directly involve action on the part of the reader. They can be as direct as instructions for actual laboratory experiments. They can be as indirect as one I recall reading in a picture book about the moon and its relationship to earth. One child was told to hold a rubber ball, standing for the moon; another, a beach ball representing the earth; and the third, a lighted lamp, the sun. As the rubber ball child and the beach ball child spin around, circling the lamp child, the beach ball experiences a kind of day and night. What could be more memorable for the child, more illuminating?

Metaphor is especially apt for scientific books. Metaphor is, after all, what science is all about. Mathematical formulae, physical models for biochemical structures—these are really metaphors for something we cannot see. Again, as Camus said about the atomic structure, "You explain this world to me with an image. . . ." It is more easily understood that way. It is explaining the unfamiliar in terms of the familiar.

Another way of dealing with information in science books is by using the aphorism. An aphorism is a short, pithy sentence or sentences that embody the truth. An aphorism is especially useful in writing about technical things for nontechnical readers. It sets the readers into a mode of thought, makes them aware of the author's intentions.

As the approach to history books for children has changed, so too the approach to scientific books for young readers has been overhauled. No longer do books say simply, "This is Truth. Learn it." The emphasis now is on showing, not telling. The child reader is given examples, ideas, and left to draw many of his own conclusions.

Some wonderful examples of science and natural science books for young readers that you should not miss are: *One Day in the Prairie* by Jean Craighead George; *Gorilla* by Robert M. McClung; *Rain of Troubles: The Science and Politics of Acid Rain* by Laurence Pringle; Franklyn Branley's "Voyage into Space" series; and *Why Doesn't the Earth Fall Up? And Other Not Such Dumb Questions about Motion* by Vicki Cobb.

How-to books

How-to books have captured their share of this audience of children. Certain publishing companies deal almost exclusively with these kinds of craft or cooking or make-and-do books; others publish an outstanding one occasionally; still other companies would not be interested in this kind of book at all. A writer interested in doing a book on a how-to subject needs to research the marketability with care. Check catalogues and library shelves. Know the publishing companies who are most keenly interested and send out query letters before actually starting on such a venture.

The keynotes to success in a how-to book are *simplicity*, *clarity*, and *precision*.

You yourself must be the guinea pig for all your instructions. You must write down exactly what you do step by step. Then you must turn about and try to follow your own instructions to the letter. Writing simple but precise instructions for what is to you the easiest task in the world, is one of the most difficult things to do. I remember working on a series of make-and-do softcover books at a publishing company I worked for. The thing that took most of our editorial time was the checking and rechecking of the directions for crafts and magic tricks. A simple half-twist in a string, an easy knot, a quick holding down of a piece of paper with a pinkie that one does without thinking about it—all these have to be explained ever so precisely to the novice. It is frustrating to detail each step, especially steps one considers common sense. But remember, in any craft what is common sense for one person may be nonsense to another.

Information into literature

It seems to me, on the whole, that there are three things to remember about nonfiction: commitment, style and the second coming, though they are rarely things that nonfiction writers mention. Yet they elevate nonfiction into the truly creative, into literature.

The very fact that we call it *non*fiction does a disservice to the genre. That puts these books in a race with fiction, indicating that they are *already* losers. Yet some of the most beautifully written information books have changed lives: *The Double Helix* (James D. Watson), *Silent Spring* (Rachel Carson), *The Soul of a New Machine* (Tracy Kidder), *The Hero with a Thousand Faces* (Joseph Campbell)—to name some special favorites of mine.

One thing these books have in common—besides the fact that they are informational in the broadest sense—is that their authors wrote them out of the deepest commitment. Not all books that impart information *have* to be written with that kind of passion, but surely a kind of fascination or a deep desire to learn more about a subject *must* be there from the start. Any slackening of interest, any boredom on the author's part will show through at once.

Style is, of course, the particular way of setting down the information gathered. It is taking the many threads and weaving a tapestry. Threads can be forgotten or overlooked. A tapestry is forever. The words in an information book can sing, can paint pictures, can be infused with a life that draws the reader in, not just the who-what-where-when-how of journalism.

For example, why say prosaically "People are so different, that any stories told about them sound like fairy tales" when you could write—as Georgess McHargue does in *The Impossible People*—"If there have been men who lived in caves and forests, grass huts and stone palaces, why not men who live in the air and under the sea?" And she draws you into her book.

In Jean Fritz's moving biography *The Double Life of Pocahontas*, she writes: "No matter how much Namontack had told the Indians about London, they could never have imagined what it was really like. Not even Pocahontas could have been prepared for this gigantic, boisterous, noisy, crowded city; horses, carriages, and carts fighting each other for room on the narrow streets; people shouting that they had scissors for sale, hot buns for sale, flowers for sale. Buy here, buy here, buy, buy, buy, they cried." The dry facts are given flesh because of Jean Fritz's style.

The most intriguing thing for me about informational books, however, is the fact of the second coming. Nothing researched is ever lost. Having spent days, weeks, months, even years inside a particular subject, it would be a shame, would it not, to get just *one* book or story out of it? What a waste of time, energy, talent, insight and knowledge. What to do? Recycle. Use it again. (See Chapter 2 for examples.)

Many kinds of books

Although we think of nonfiction books as one familiar kind of book—straightforward reportage—there are many different ways to write a book for young readers that will give them information.

Nonfiction picture books may be in story form, like Jim Murphy's brilliant *The Last Dinosaur* or Alice and Martin

Provenson's Caldecott-winning *The Glorious Flight*, in which the information is embedded in the body of the story. They may be amusingly presented in a picture book format that has characters mouthing facts, as in Tomie de Paola's charming *The Quicksand Book*. They may even be in an easy-reading format. Harper & Row has both an *I Can Read Science* series and an *I Can Read History* series, and will send style sheets for would-be authors on request.

So, too, books for older readers can be straightforward and factual, the invitation to learning given as much by the well-designed format (photographs and period drawings as in the Freedman biography of Lincoln) as by interesting marginalia (as in my book *Ring Out!*, about bells) or other typographically intriguing ideas.

They can also be in story form, following the biography as if watching a fascinating tale unfold. Rhoda Blumberg's *Commodore Perry in the Land of the Shōgun* is one such. Jean Fritz's delightful books about history such as *Why Don't You Get A Horse, Sam Adams?* and her *Who's That Stepping on Plymouth Rock* are absolutely accurate while gently poking fun at the very human makers of history.

This final word about nonfiction books is a cautionary one. As we saw in the beginning of this chapter and must be reminded of again in the end, "just the facts, ma'am" is not enough. The importance of nonfiction trade books for children of the twentieth century cannot be too heavily underscored. It is not only that children are little sponges absorbing every bit of specific information that comes their way. It is also, in Huxley's words, that "every concrete particular, public or private, is a window opening onto the universal."

We must give the children we are writing for not only data—the particular—but also a little boost into the universal—with information.

*Human beings are often liable to conde-
scend to other animals, whose lives are
often better organized than their own.*
                                —T. H. White

‖ 10

Animal Tales (or Thereby Hangs a Tail)

I N THE FIELD OF CHILDREN'S BOOKS, the animal story has
always reigned supreme. In fact, mention to most
adults that you are writing a children's book, and they will
immediately think of teddy bears, soft bunnies, and other
animals of the "cuddly" set. Or even if the animal is too
large to cuddle (like Munro Leaf's bull Ferdinand or Anne
McCaffrey's dragons), there are extenuating circumstances
that make the animal pettable, even if it is not immediately
cuddly.

But in fact most animals found in children's books are not
of the cuddly or pettable variety. There are three distinct
categories of animal books: *talking* animal stories, *realistic*
animal stories, and *scientific* animal stories.

Tales about animals are among the oldest stories in existence. In those once-upon-a-time days when people told

stories around campfires, it was the animal who was the conveyor of truth or the trickster god or the pointer of morals (à la Aesop). Animals like Raven and Coyote and Anansi the Spider had entire story cycles told about them.

So the first "authors" to use animals in their stories were the primitive oral tellers. From there to the medieval fabliaux was but a short step from Aesop. Bestiaries added to the known animals, mixing the real and unreal with fantastic abandon. By the 17th century and La Fontaine, animal stories had left behind their innocence and had become straight satirical tales.

When Anna Sewell wrote *Black Beauty* in 1877, with great didactic and philanthropic intent, a new kind of animal story was born—the realistic animal tale. No longer were animal stories merely a means to clothe humankind's foibles in fur and feathers. In Sewell's horrific story of the maltreatment of a horse, there was no doubt which was the cruel beast. It was man who was ignoble and the horse saintly and long (very long) suffering.

Close on the heels of *Black Beauty*, the third strain of animal story was developed when Sir Charles G. D. Roberts wrote *Earth Enigmas*. His stories were supra-realistic and often excluded any human characters at all. In the Roberts tales, the animals are motivated by habit and instinct, not by greed or power, vanity, shyness, or love. Although no one reads Sir Charles today, there are many naturalistic animal writers who have benefitted from his invention: Robert M. McClung, Berniece Freschet, Faith McNulty, to name just three.

Animal tales in general are probably the single largest category in children's books. The animal story spans all ages—from the tiniest picture book to full-length novels. There are no publishers who do not have a horse or dog book somewhere on their present or past lists; usually several of both. And besides dogs and horses, the inevitable dinosaur, bear, pig, and owl books.

Talking animal stories

The talking animal book is the delight of young readers and—alas—the bane of most editors' existence, because as appealing as they are for children, they are very difficult to write. Most of the time, the manuscripts with talking animals that find their way into an editor's hands suffer terribly from the "cutes," or what author Tomie de Paola calls "the bunny-wunny, ducky-wucky syndrome."

Children respond to talking animal stories the way they do to any folktale. From the writer's point of view, these books must abide by the rules of the fairy and fantasy tale, though the animals are responding as prototypical humans.

If you want to write about an animal that has recognizably human feelings and emotional responses, you must realize from the start that you are writing a fantasy story. If, as T. H. White claims, animals' lives are better organized than our own, it is on a simpler scale: direct responses to stimuli rather than the tortuous mind-turnings of humans.

Even if your fantasy animal talks, keep one thing in mind: No matter how well it enunciates its words or how deep its emotions, you must pay attention to its animal size or shape or animal uniqueness. For example, if it is a hitchhiking toad—as in my novel *Hobo Toad and the Motorcycle Gang*—it cannot suddenly fly. In that story, the toad saves the day by using his marvelous tongue, so adept at catching flies, to untie the knots in the ropes that bind his companions. If the story is about a spider, as in E. B. White's *Charlotte's Web*, she saves a friend's life by spinning messages in her web.

The first question a writer must ask before embarking on a talking animal story is, "Is the animal necessary to the tale?" If the answer is, "Because an animal is cuter," or "I just felt like putting one there," it is time to rethink your premise.

Take a look at some of the great talking animal stories: *Peter Rabbit* by Beatrix Potter; *The Wind in the Willows* by Kenneth Grahame; *The Jungle Book* by Rudyard Kipling; *Charlotte's Web* by E. B. White; *Watership Down* by Richard Adams. It is necessary for those animals to talk. Besides, they avoid the three major traps of this kind of book—triviality, sentimentality, and excessive melodrama.

Realistic animal stories

The second kind of animal book is the realistic animal book that began with *Black Beauty* and went through Jack London, Albert Terhune, and Walter Farley. In these novels, the animals' hearts break as regularly as clockwork.

Realistic to a point, these animals do not wear clothes or mess about in boats. They growl or grunt or gobble, rather than talk. Yet, because the authors are romantics at heart, they endow their animal characters with recognizable human emotions.

In the realistic animal story, the animal may be a hero like *Bob, Son of Battle* (Alfred Ollivant), or an anti-hero like *Old One-Toe* (Michel-Aimé Baudouy), or a super-hero like *The Black Stallion* (Walter Farley). But these episodic adventure stories have one thing in common—a noble and often suffering (at the hands of man) animal. What might sound trite or overly sentimental in a story about people can be rationalized in a realistic animal tale.

The keynote for this kind of book is plot: fast-paced adventures tumbling over one another, hair-breadth escapes, and at least the outward appearance of realism.

Scientific animal stories

The scientific animal story is comparatively new and should be attempted only by authors who really understand animal life. Often the best authors of this kind of story are zoologists, biologists, veterinarians, animal breeders, or ardent wildlife observers. For example, Sterling North actually raised the raccoon *Rascal* that he wrote about. Robert M. McClung was a curator for the Bronx Zoo and keeper of a terrarium full of caterpillars when he wrote *Sphinx: The Story of a Caterpillar.* And David Stemple spent many years observing wild turkeys in the fields of Massachusetts, New York, Vermont, and West Virginia before writing *High Ridge Gobbler: A Story of the American Wild Turkey.*

Sometimes in these scientific animal stories, the actual events are true and reported exactly, as in Joy Adamson's *Born Free.*

But *Sphinx* is a composite of a number of caterpillars that McClung observed.

The success of these stories sometimes depends on the obscurity of the animal. In a market satiated with cats and dogs, the real life story of a star-nosed mole, a vampire bat, or a harpy eagle might more readily find a publisher and audience.

The animal story ranges from the talking lion lying down with the talking lamb, to the scientifically described lion devouring its woolly companion. And after twenty successive talking-kitty manuscripts, the editor might well refuse even to look at another anthropomorphic story, whether the animal talks and walks on two feet or is presented with scientific accuracy. In general, it is best to query before submitting your animal story.

The world is wide. Everything in it can be used to make books for children.
—Taro Yashima

‖ 11

The Functions of Form

WHEN I FIRST BEGAN WRITING for children, I inadvertently came upon a "word list" put out by a publishing company and sent on request to would-be authors. On two pages printed in very large type, it contained what that publishing house (in conjunction with the best educators of the day) considered the entire beginning reader's vocabulary allowed in first books: 361 words. For the "beginning" beginner (whatever that meant!), the list was a mere 181 words.

The introduction to the list spelled out this particular publisher's ground rules for writing books for beginning readers. The publisher claimed that these were words that first-graders already knew by sight. Authors were warned against *-ed*, *-ing*, and *-er* endings, and were cautioned against using contractions. They were absolutely forbidden to use possessives.

I puzzled over the 361 words for a long time, trying to imagine the kind of story I might write with such a restrictive vocabulary, feeling like a potter asked to make a salad bowl with an ounce of clay, or a woodworker ordered to create a table out of a splinter.

I came up with nothing. Nothing at all.

There was always the possibility that I was lacking in imagination, and so I turned in my frustration to that master of imaginative sense and nonsense, Lewis Carroll.

The first page of *Alice in Wonderland* goes:

> Alice was beginning to get very tired of sitting by her sister on the bank, and of having nothing to do; once or twice she had peeped into the book her sister was reading, but it had no pictures or conversation in it, "and what is the use of a book," thought Alice, "without pictures or conversation."

Clearly, that would never do. In it, there were over twenty words not sanctioned by the list, not to mention perfectly good words ruined by *-ed* and *-ing* endings. *Alice* was obviously not for today's young readers!

But I remembered vividly my first reading of *Alice*: I was six years old, and I had to ask my mother about a lot of the words, but I had loved the book.

I knew that, given the proper vocabulary, children in the second half of the twentieth century would love the book if I could remove any offending words.

> Alice was to get very of sit by her on the, end of no thing to do; once or she had into the book her was read, but it had no or in it, "and what is the of a book," thought Alice, "with out or."

Heavens—jabberwocky!

My duty was clear. To render *Alice* readable for young readers today, I must not simply delete words, but would have to rewrite the classic, substituting only the approved words for any of the forbidden vocabulary.

Alice began to get very sleepy as she sat by her mother by the water with not a thing to do. One or two times she had looked into the book her mother read, but it had no paint or talk in it, "and what good is a book," thought Alice, "with no paint or talk."

Certainly it was now readable. Even understandable. A few sleights-of-hand had occurred. *Mother* had replaced *sister* by Alice's side. To foreshadow the dream, I used *sleepy* instead of *tired*. And that odd substitution of *paint and talk* for *pictures and conversation* should not trouble any but the most rigidly purist soul.

Yet what was missing? What was lost in my translation? Style, fluidity of language, the poetry of the line, and occasionally even the intent of the author. In my version, the child's eye and ear would get poor change for their book coin. That is what happens any time you try to write a book with a prescribed or proscribed vocabulary.

And what is a vocabulary list anyway? In *The New England Primer* there is a list of words for young Puritan readers that includes *fornication, vile,* and *sloth*. None of those words is within a country mile of my twentieth-century list. So a proscribed vocabulary has something to do with easy words and something to do with moral lessons.

At a time in a child's life when he or she is learning approximately 20 new words a day (what adolescent or adult given words to memorize can make that claim?), writers (and publishers) must not limit their young readers' vocabulary.

The classic example of the idiocy of "word leveling," written by children's book editor Ann Durell, was read at an American Library Association meeting some years ago. It was a marvelously vicious parody of easy-reading versions, based on the classic: *Jane Eyre.*

This is Jane.
Hello Jane.
Jane is poor.
Her dress is poor.
Her shoes are poor.
Her hat is poor.
Poor Jane.

This is Mr. Rochester.
Hello Mr. Rochester.
Mr. Rochester is rich.
He has a big house.
He has a big dog.
He has a big horse.
He has a big secret.
What is Mr. Rochester's secret?
Jane cannot guess the secret,
Can you guess the secret?

This is Mrs. Rochester.
Hello Mrs. Rochester.
Mrs. Rochester is crazy.
She has a candle.
The candle is lighted.
Mrs. Rochester can laugh.
She laughs: ha ha ha.
RUN JANE RUN.

No one would do *that* to a classic. Yet just in the past
couple of years, a British edition of *Peter Rabbit* was published, rewritten in easy language (gone are *scuttered* and
exert) and illustrated with photographs of rabbit puppets.
Similarly, George MacDonald's *The Light Princess* was cut
down to fit into a picture book format. *Black Beauty* was
rewritten in an easier-to-read style. Textbook companies
perpetuate this kind of damage by having *Don Quixote*
rewritten for fifth-graders and changing the vocabulary in

poetry and other literary works to suit their prescribed lists.

For example, my Caldecott Honor Book *The Emperor and the Kite* has been reprinted a number of times in textbooks. In the story, there is a haiku which goes:

> My kite sails upward,
> Mounting to the high heavens.
> My soul goes on wings.

It is spoken by a monk who does not otherwise talk.

Over the years I have resisted textbook firms who have wanted to change that last line to *My spirit goes on wings* or *My karma goes on wings* and even *My life force goes on wings*.

My advice to writers' perennial questions about the proper vocabulary for a children's book is this: Use the right word for the right occasion, whether it is a one-letter, two-letter, three-letter or twenty-four letter word. If the child already knows the word, there is no problem. A child who speaks already has a vocabulary of thousands of words. And if the child has to learn a new word, so much the better.

Easy reading breath spaces

Having said all that, I have to admit there is a particular type of book, very popular in the 1970s and coming back into fashion, known as the *Easy Reader.*

These are books written in shorter sentences, and while the vocabulary is not controlled, the words tend to be those more easily comprehended by a new reader. (Keep in mind, though, that today's six-year-old can more easily read and understand the familiar *brontosaurus*, than he can *slough*.)

Many publishers have specific series of easy-reading books: Harper & Row has its *I Can Read* books imprint,

Dial has an *Easy-to-Read Books* series, Dutton has *Easy Readers*, and *Little Critter Easy Readers* are published by Golden Books.

What these books have in common is that they are specifically aimed at the boys and girls who have just broken the reading code and want to read something *interesting*.

The best of the easy readers are not only interesting, they are lively reading: Arnold Lobel's *Frog and Toad* books, Betty Boegehold's *Pippa Mouse* books, the Hobans' *Frances Badger* books, Sue Alexander's *Witch, Goblin, Ghost* stories, and of course the ever-popular *Little Bear* books by Else Minarik.

An important trick of the easy-reading trade is writing in "breath spaces." Once children can sound out letters and read words, the next hardest thing for them to do is to make sense of the sentences. They don't know yet that commas, semi-colons, and periods signify pauses of varying lengths. Any group of words sitting together on a page looks like a phrase, and if the phrase they see goes like this:

> Jack and Jill went up

they read it just that way, pausing at the end. If you write in "breath spaces," breaking a phrase where it should be broken, the young reader begins to understand the rhythm of sentences intuitively.

When I write easy-reading books, like my *Commander Toad* series, I set the story on the page as if it were a poem, writing in those breath space phrases that invite the child to read it correctly:

> Long ships fly
> between the stars.
> Outside each porthole
> worlds wink off and on.
> There is one ship,

one mighty ship,
long and green,
that goes across the skies.

Even though it has some very "big" words—*porthole* and *outside* and later on some even bigger ones like *commander, lieutenant, galaxies,* and *alien*—they are all outer space words. Children who enjoy science fiction adventures will have no trouble with the vocabulary. I have heard from hundreds of grateful parents and teachers who tell me how their children began reading with *Commander Toad.*

Paperbacks bring readers back

In the days of the chapbooks—tales like *Jack the Giant Killer* bound in paper and sold for a penny—a determined child reader might sneak one home, as he later did with comic books.

In the 1960s and 1970s, paperback reprints for children began to appear. But, original paperbacks for children are relatively new. What was once simply a reprint market has now become a solid market for original material, for which writers can and should target their work. Because price is an important consideration for publishers of paperbacks, the paper, binding, and inks are less costly, and consequently, the books are much less durable. For this reason, libraries initially were very slow to order paperbacks in quantity (and often did not even put them through the regular cataloguing process). But as the demand grew, availability of titles and quality grew, too. Over the past twenty-five years, increasing numbers of hardback publishers have been bringing out paperback originals, not just reprints of softbound books (another term used for them). In fact, almost every major children's book publisher has or is in the process of developing a line of children's paperbacks. Dell was a pioneer in the field. Its Yearling Books for younger readers and its Laurel Leaf line for older ones are very popular. *Charlotte's Web*, a Yearling reprint, has sold well over a million copies.

The newest direction for young people's paperback originals are in series (the most successful of which are Sweet Valley High, and The Babysitter Club books) a recent phenomenon that has made some publishers, some authors, and some agents very rich. What the books lack in literary values, they more than make up for in sales.

The magazine market

From 1873 to 1940 there lived (in Boston) a publishing phenomenon known as *St. Nicholas*, a magazine for children edited for 25 years by Mary Mapes Dodge. In its heyday it published such authors as Louisa May Alcott, Frank Stockton, L. Frank Baum, Bret Harte, Frances Hodgson Burnett, Joel Chandler Harris, and many other literary luminaries. In its pages many children's classics first saw light: Kipling's *The Jungle Book*, Lucretia Hale's *The Peterkin Papers*, Mary Mapes Dodge's *Hans Brinker, or the Silver Skates*, Howard Pyle's *King Arthur*, Joel Harris's *Uncle Remus* stories, Alcott's *Under the Lilacs* and *Jack and Jill*, among others. (As a child, Edna St. Vincent Millay had her first poem published there.)

Since that time many other magazines for young readers have been published, but none has ever achieved the level of wit, style, literacy, or the fantastic examples of pure genius—and the popularity—of *St. Nicholas*.

Nowadays, children's magazines seem to follow a style best described as Late Eclectic: a few stories, a factual article or two, a few poems (usually of the jingly verse variety), a learning game, some crafts or things-to-do, a simple-minded song about manners or morals, and some puzzles or riddles.

There are literally hundreds of magazines being published for young readers today, and they fall into three categories: *secular, religious* (the largest category), and *specialized.* All of the magazine editors encourage would-be contributors to study several copies of the magazine before submitting; many have guidelines, usually available on request, with a self-addressed, stamped envelope— (SASE). The guidelines are invaluable to help you submit work that is appropriate to the magazine's specific editorial focus and requirements. As you analyze the magazines you wish to write for, see if there is a particular slant to the articles, stories, or poems. Are they long or short? Does the magazine have a recognizable style? Is the kind of material you write suitable in content and format?

These magazines often will buy *all rights* to a manuscript. That means that they—and *not you*—will benefit if the piece is reprinted in another magazine or a textbook or is made into a storybook, for a fee; be sure you understand what it is you are selling. If possible, sell only first publication rights, retaining all future rights so *you* get the fee or share it.

There are a number of ways to find out the names and addresses of the many magazines for young readers. *The Writer* Magazine lists publications for children in its April issue, and in its annual reference book, *The Writer's Handbook.* A *Children's Magazine Guide,* published monthly and found in most large public libraries, lists the articles found in all the children's magazines. If you are a member of the Society of Children's Book Writers, you can send for its *Directory Guide to Magazine Markets.*

Started in 1968 by two young writers looking for a group

to join, SCBW now has over 4,600 members, including novices as well as today's top authors and illustrators of children's books.

SCBW holds regional meetings and critique workshops; runs a national conference annually; sends out a bimonthly newsletter; gives grants for works-in-progress, of fiction, nonfiction, and illustration; awards the Golden Kite to the best children's books in fiction, nonfiction, and illustration; has a number of informative pamphlets and brochures on a variety of important subjects—specific markets, contracts, agents, and preparing manuscripts for publication, among others.

For membership application and qualifications, write to SCBW, P.O. Box 296, Mar Vista Station, Los Angeles, CA 90066.

The following are among the most widely read and popular magazines for young readers today, including their addresses and submission requirements:

Cobblestone (ages 8–14) 20 Grove St., Peterborough, NH 03458. A history magazine that uses stories and articles, up to 1,200 words, and poems on specific themes. A list of themes for upcoming issues is available; enclose self-addressed, stamped envelope. Pays to 15¢ a word, on publication.

Cricket (ages 6–12) Open Court Publishing Co., Box 300, Peru, IL 61301. Uses stories and articles, 200 to 1,500 words, and poetry to 30 lines. Payment is to 25¢ a word, and to $3 a line for poetry, on publication.

Highlights for Children (ages 2–12) 803 Church St., Honesdale, PA 18431. Uses fiction with strong plots and articles, to 900 words. Humor and stories about struggle or self-sacrifice preferred. Pays 8¢ a word, on publication.

Humpty Dumpty's Magazine (ages 4–6) 1100 Waterway Blvd., P.O. Box 567, Indianapolis, IN 46206. Easy-to-read fiction, to 600 words, some with health, nutrition, safety, exercise, or hygiene theme; humor and light approach preferred. Short verse and narrative poems. Payment is 8¢ a word, from $10 for poems, on publication.

Jack and Jill (ages 6–8) Box 567, Indianapolis, IN 46206. Articles, 500 to 1,000 words, on sports, nature, safety, etc., and features, 1,000 to 1,200 words, on history, biography, life in other countries. Fiction to 1,000 words. Short poems. Pays 8¢ a word, on publication.

Ranger Rick (ages 6–12) 1412 16th St. N.W., Washington, DC 20036. Fiction and nonfiction, to 900 words, on any aspect of nature, environment, conservation, or the natural sciences. Pays to $350, on acceptance.

*Each good book calls forth a different re-
sponse from an editor.*

—Jean Karl

‖ 12

Into the Marketplace

T HE MOMENT OF TRUTH is at hand. You have finished
your manuscript, revised it any number of times, typed
it in proper double-spaced format and made at least one
copy. Now you are ready to ship it off. But to whom?

Do you send it to the very first name on the list of
children's book publishers? Or do you start, for luck, at the
end? Do you send it to any particular editor or the publisher or To Whom it May Concern? Do you try for an agent
first?

Following these marketing basics will save you time,
money, and a great deal of anxiety.

The ABCs of publishing

Unless you are writing specifically for your desk drawer,
you need to acquaint yourself with the wide and deep world
of that market pool.

Should you be looking for a major publisher? A small
press? A regional publisher? A religious house? Are there

contests you might enter or grants you might apply for? These are only the opening questions you must answer before you are *really* ready to send your manuscript on its way.

First, though, you must know—and believe—that no matter where you send your manuscript, someone—a first reader, assistant editor, or editor—will at least start to read your manuscript unless the publisher has a stated policy that it is no longer reading manuscripts or wants to see a query, outline, or summary first.

Even if you send your manuscript with a two-page cover letter, a one-paragraph cover letter, or no letter at all, it will be directed to the appropriate person. But *always* try to address your query or manuscript to an editor by name at the publication or publisher. (Look on the masthead of the magazine or in the listings in *Literary Market Place*, *The Writer*, or *The Writer's Handbook*.) If the manuscript seems from the beginning to be unsuitable, it will be returned if you send sufficient postage on a self-addressed, stamped envelope.

Editors know that authors are the lifeblood of publishing. Without authors, there would be no books. BUT there are many ways to *read* or *handle* a manuscript. And there are many ways to accept and/or reject a manuscript. You must send out your manuscript in a way that will at least increase the chances of its being considered by the most qualified person in the shortest amount of time with the least amount of heartbreak for you. That is no small order.

Catalogues and other market reports

Book publishers' catalogues provide a wealth of information. Most companies produce seasonal (spring and fall) catalogues, including lists and descriptions of their new or forthcoming titles as well as their backlists. The promotion department will usually send you their newest catalogues on request. Or you can go to your local bookstore or library and browse through catalogues they may have on file.

Catalogues will tell you what kind of books a particular company regularly publishes. For example, except for one or two YA novels, Franklin Watts does not publish fiction, but its imprint Orchard Books does. Delacorte, which has one of the top YA lines, does not produce picture books. A careful reading of the catalogues will also tell you which companies regularly publish fantasy novels or historicals, which seem uninterested in read-alouds, which have series of biographies. You will also get an idea of the size of the company: fewer than twenty new books a publishing season indicates a small list (Holiday House, Farrar, Straus & Giroux), over thirty indicates a large house (Harper & Row, Harcourt Brace Jovanovich, Putnam's). You will also find out if there have been recent books that cover the same subject as yours, in fiction, nonfiction, or whatever. A company that has just released a biography of John F. Kennedy, for example, or a book about bells, or a novel set in Detroit in the Depression or a picture book on the changing seasons is not likely to want a similar one immediately. However, just because a company has recently published a fantasy book about a mouse or a picture book about a girl in a nursery school does not automatically rule out their considering your fantasy novel about a mole or your picture book about a boy in kindergarten.

- The catalogues are not the only shortcuts to understanding the market. There are a number of publications that are useful, too, and can be found in most libraries: *The Horn Book, Publishers Weekly, School Library Journal, Parents' Choice, The Writer,* and *The*

New York Times Book Review are some of the ones to check out.

- *The Horn Book*, a magazine that specializes in children's books, comes out six times a year and is chock full of reviews and articles by critics, authors, librarians, teachers, illustrators, and some bookstore owners; the magazine also carries ads from publishers. *The Horn Book* is at 14 Beacon St., Boston, MA 02108.

- *Publishers Weekly*, a magazine for the publishing trade, runs short reviews of children's books. Twice a year it devotes a full issue to the children's book field. *School Library Journal* is entirely oriented to public, private, and school libaries that, of course, cater to school-age readers. The reviewers are librarians, and they evaluate the books in terms of their suitability to such libraries.

    Since bookstore sales play only a small part in children's book sales—though there are now over 300 stores devoted entirely to children's books—and 70% of a book's sales will be to the institutional markets (schools and libraries), it is important for writers to consult both of these magazines. By keeping an eye on books favorably reviewed and reading them as models, by noting which publishers—and libraries—are looking for books, by understanding what pressures are being brought to bear on children's book publishing, the writer goes armored into the marketplace. *Publishers Weekly* and *School Library Journal* are published by Bowker Publishing Co., 249 W. 17th Street, New York 10011.

• *Parents' Choice* is a tabloid-sized paper that comes out six times a year with reviews of and articles about books and other media for children. There are other equally good small magazines covering some of the same subjects *(The Five Owls, Kinderbook, The New Advocate)*, but their track records are a great deal shorter than *Parents' Choice* (1191 Chestnut St., Newton, MA 02164).

Another excellent source of information is the Children's Book Council, 67 Irving Place, New York, NY 10003. Their monthly "Calendar" is a gold mine of assorted subjects, with information about publishers, authors, and books. CBC is the parent council for all children's book publishers and produces an updated list of its members each year (sent upon request with the enclosure of a SASE). For those who are members, the best single source of information is the Society of Children's Book Writers, discussed in Chapter 11.

To query or not to query

After studying the market, it is often a good idea to send a query letter to the publisher or magazine to which you plan to submit your book. A query letter is a shortcut and will be answered in a relatively short time—possibly days, certainly no more than a few weeks. (Manuscripts are quite often kept months before being rejected . . .or accepted.) Many book publishers *require* queries and will not read unsolicited manuscripts. This is especially time-saving for a nonfiction project or a historical or period novel, an adventure story, or a specific sports story. After all, an editor will not want to take on a project too similar to one already published or in the works. Also, he or she may judge from your query whether your proposed work is one they wish to consider.

A simple query letter might look like this:

Dear *(editor's name):*

I am working on a book about the history and lore of bells tentatively entitled, *Ring Out: A Book of Bells.* It is for the 8–12 age group and will include stories and songs about bells as well as historical material.

There are only eight books on bells in print today, of which two are children's books. Those two are for a much younger audience than the book I am writing.

My writing background includes a number of published magazine and newspaper articles.

If you are interested, I would be pleased to send you a full outline and sample of my proposed book.

Sincerely,

This kind of letter is sure to elicit a quick response from an editor. It introduces the book topic simply and without being cute. (No "This is not a book for ding-a-lings." Or "I hope this rings a bell with you!") It outlines the probable competition. It specifies the writer's expertise (or specific familiarity with the material). And finally, it mentions that there is material completed for the editor to read.

Query letters may be sent off to any number of editors at the same time, unlike manuscripts; many editors still resist the idea of multiple submissions. One warning: There are also some editors who object to multiple queries, but there are certainly fewer than in the past. You may judge the editors' degree of interest from their responses: Which one seems most sympathetic to your proposal? Which one seems most eager to read it? Which ones seem lukewarm to the idea? Which ones say no? Rank the responses and then get your manuscript in the mail, beginning with the most serious and excited editor.

As invaluable as query letters are for writers, there are certain kinds of books that are really impossible to query about.

Can you imagine the kind of query letter Miss Beatrix Potter might send?

> Dear Sirs:
> Although I am a maiden lady and have no children of my own, I have decided to fashion a little book about a particular rabbit friend of mine, a naughty little bunny who disobeys his Mother and goes into Farmer McGregor's garden.
> I have decorated the book with my own drawings from life and call my little book *Peter Rabbit.* Are you interested?
> Sincerely,
Beatrix Potter

In such instances, of course, query letters are worse than useless. They cannot give the flavor, style, or feeling of a book and, in the case of many picture books, the query letter would be longer than the book itself.

If you receive a "go-ahead" to your query directly from a particular editor, address your manuscript to that editor by name, as that person will most likely remember your query and will look forward to receiving and reading the manuscript.

Rules for submission

When you submit your manuscript, remember these six important rules.

1. *Always type the manuscript* double-spaced on good bond (20 lb.) paper, whether it is a picture storybook or a 200-page novel. Editors read hundreds of manuscripts every year and will not take time to try to decipher a handwritten manuscript or letter. Not typed, not read is the rule. Leave wide margins on all sides; make sure the

type is dark enough to be readable, and do not use any fancy fonts, which are difficult to read. Also, be sure that your manuscript has as few corrections and scribbled inserts as possible. The point is that the unprofessional look of your manuscript will turn the editor against your book from the beginning. If you use a word processor, make sure that you do not use dot matrix or fancy fonts.

2. *Be sure your name and address are on the title page.* Number your pages consecutively, with your name in the upper corner of each page. This sounds like an idiot's rule, but many authors forget it. If by accident a manuscript is dropped (and with an editor handling so many manuscripts a year, it is a certainty that at least *one* manuscript will be dropped! Murphy's Law guarantees that *it will always be the unnumbered manuscript*), if it is numbered and named, reassembling it will not be a problem.

3. *Always keep a copy of your finished manuscript.* Two are preferable, one in a safe, fireproof place. I know many new writers who are so eager to get their manuscripts off to an editor, they don't make a copy of the *final* copy.

4. *Keep a card file of your manuscript's travels* so that you do not inadvertently send it again to the same publisher. You may *think* that you can keep all this in your head, but if you have sent it out ten times, or have more than one manuscript making the rounds, it will be impossible to remember all of the details. Each round trip almost always entails from one to three months.

5. *Do not submit the same manuscript to more than one publisher at the same time.* Multiple submissions are still absolutely out! The reason publishers do not like multiple submissions is that they spend valuable time and money reading, evaluating, and then costing out books they are interested in. If, after all that, they discover that you have

been negotiating with another company, they will react negatively to anything you submit in the future.

6. *A cover letter is not necessary, but it is polite to include a short one.* Remember the corollary: *less is more.* The shorter, the better. And omit *extraneous* biographical material, but do include publishing credits or information about your profession, if relevant; i.e., if you are a teacher, a librarian, or are famous in the field you are writing about.

Do you need an agent?

"How do I get an agent?" That is the most frequently asked question at gatherings of writers. The problem is that there are very few agents who really know the children's book field, and few, if any, will read the work of unpublished writers. Find out the names of those who might be willing to look at your material. If you are a member of the Society of Children's Book Writers, write for their brochure on agents. There is also a list available from the Society of Authors Representatives, 39½ Washington Sq. South, New York, NY 10012. Author Aid/Research Associates (340 E. 52nd St., New York, NY 10022) publishes a book entitled *Literary Agents of North America Marketplace,* and Poets & Writers (201 W. 54th St., New York, NY 10019) publishes *Literary Agents, A Writer's Guide.*

Be wary of agents who advertise or charge a reading fee. Their aim is to make money *from* the author, not *for* the author. Legitimate agents are paid only a percentage of the royalties they receive from the publisher of *your work.*

The answer to the question, "Is an agent necessary?" is "no"—not unless you feel you need one. Then, having an agent is indispensable. Although I have one, many famous and successful authors do not. There are authors who swear by their agents—and others who swear *at* them. Often they are talking about the same agent.

An agent can be an entree into certain publishing companies that no longer read unsolicited manuscripts. An agent can be your business advisor. An agent will be your ombudsman. An agent *can be* your most fervent supporter and literary friend. That is what my agent is to me, but I sold my first four books before I met her.

Good agents are on top of the publishing scene, following it on a daily basis. They keep track of editors who have moved to new companies and will know an editor's special likes and dislikes, a company's current needs, which companies are the most reputable, which produce the most attractive books, have the best sales and distribution staff. They know from experience the publishers who treat their authors with the most respect, spend money on advertising and promotion, and are trustworthy in all their financial dealings. Agents often have connections with European publishers, movie companies, TV studios, radio producers, record companies; they understand the fine print on a contract and will fight for the highest advance and royalty terms, the best secondary rights split.

Of course, authors themselves can become knowledgeable in all these areas. By reading the trade magazines, going to writers conferences, keeping carefully annotated files on the comings and goings of editors and publishers, perusing the catalogues, asking the right questions, having a lawyer go over any contracts (though this requires specialized legal experience), and talking to published authors, a new writer can shepherd his or her work through the publishing process. Because an agent takes 10% to 15%. Of everything you get for what is sold.

The editorial process

Once the manuscript is on its way to the publishing house, begin immediately on your next story or book or poem. That is the professional approach. As Phyllis

Whitney so aptly put it: "No vacations between stories." If you are working hard on something else, you will never stand at the mailbox waiting to hear from the publisher.

It is going to take a long time for the publisher to respond: anywhere from six weeks to four months. This is why:

When your manuscript reaches a publishing company, it is logged in, either by a secretary, a manuscript clerk, or an assistant editor. Sometimes (though rarely nowadays), you will receive a postcard stating that the manuscript has been received. The manuscript is then placed in one of three piles.

If it is a manuscript from one of the editor's own authors, or a book already contracted for, or from a famous author published elsewhere who is looking for a new house, it goes in pile number one. That pile will be read by the editor within a matter of days, or at the most, weeks.

If a manuscript is sent in by a respected agent or from a published (though not famous) author, or if it has been recommended by someone the editor knows and respects, it goes into pile number two. Though this pile is usually read first by an assistant editor, an in-house manuscript reader, or an outside reader, it will have a thorough reading and a thorough report will be written on it. It may be a short pithy paragraph such as: "A tale about two monkeys in Jataka who outwit a crocodile. It is based on an old Indian folk motif. Author is Indian and has written this with wit and style. Suggest second reading." Or the report may run several pages, along with suggested revisions. Then the editor reads the manuscript, keeping in mind the first reader's report.

The third pile is called the *slush* pile—short for "unsolicited." All the manuscripts without any significant "pedigrees" attached, go into pile number three.

Into the slush pile went my very first attempt at a children's book, *Willoby the Whale Who Wanted to be a Minnow*, which I now understand was one of the editors' pet aversions—talking defective animal with an alliterative name. It deserved what it got!

Make no mistake: all manuscripts, even those in the slush pile, are read, or at least looked at, to the degree they merit. Good slush pile stories *will* get a second reading, *will* be passed on up to the top editor. Every year there are some books published from the slush piles of publishing companies, like Nancy Bond's *A String in the Harp*, which was accepted, published, and awarded a Newbery Honor.

The slush pile manuscripts are the ones that most often receive printed rejection notes that tell the author absolutely nothing about how close or far away the story was from acceptance.

You must understand, too, why it takes so long to hear either yes or no on your manuscript. Reading manuscripts is something editors do at home in the evenings and on weekends. I do not know a single editor who does not take piles of manuscripts home every single day. Office time consists of meetings; answering mail and phone calls; dealing with the day-to-day problems in running a business; consulting with the art, sales, and promotion departments; reading galleys; writing flap copy; viewing artist portfolios; and seeing visiting authors, illustrators, and overseas publishers. There is no time left to read manuscripts—except at home.

If you receive neither a rejection nor an acceptance letter in six weeks, you can write a polite, nudging letter to the editor. By two months, you can send a slightly stronger letter. By three, make a telephone call. By four send a registered letter of inquiry. If that brings no response, you can consider sending a letter withdrawing the manuscript and then feel free to send it to another publisher.

There is usually no reason for an editor to take more than

two to three months to read a simple manuscript, especially if it is only a few pages long. However, do not mistake the amount of time taken for genuine interest in your manuscript. Sometimes it is true that the company is busily figuring out a way to publish it. Just as often, though, they have been too busy to read your book and that is why it has taken so long. Rule of thumb: *time does not equal interest— necessarily.*

How to read a rejection letter

Do not be discouraged by one or two or more rejection letters. After 100 published books, I still get rejections. My Caldecott-winning book *Owl Moon* was turned down two times. My Caldecott Honor Book *The Emperor and the Kite* was turned down six times. My best-selling *Sleeping Ugly* was turned down thirteen times. I have a nonfiction project I have been trying to sell for fifteen years. Madeleine L'Engle's Newbery winner *A Wrinkle in Time* was rejected by thirty publishing houses. Almost every author can tell you a similar story.

The point is not to be discouraged—but at the same time to be realistic. After the first five rejection letters, reread the book and ask yourself that most difficult question: Are they right? If your answer is an objective no, then be ready to send it out another five times. If you are being honest with yourself and you have a solid basis for your belief (you have educated yourself in the genre, your manuscript will eventually find its editor.

Reading your rejection letters is a science and an art. Of course, if you receive a printed form letter, it is useless to guess what it means. It *could* be that your manuscript really is no good at all. It could be that your book is too similar to another on the publisher's list. (Reading the catalogue would have helped here.) It could be that the publisher does not publish this kind of book. (You did not do your homework.) Or any number of other reasons, such as an editor's personal bias, or that, in a publisher's opinion, the market for that particular type of book has dried up.

But if the editor has taken time to scribble a few words on the printed form like "Close" or "Try us again"—you should certainly feel encouraged. Editors do not arbitrarily take time to comment to unknown authors, or to those they consider unsalvageable. If they write a comment on the rejection slip, it is precisely because they wish to encourage you.

If you receive a personalized rejection of any kind it means your manuscript was considered seriously, or the editors felt they owed you an explanation (a well-known educator or a published author, for example, might receive personalized attention). When you receive this kind of letter, you may have to read between the lines.

- *Not right for our list* is one of those pat phrases that can mean an editor is more interested in the writer than in that particular book. However, it has come to mean little more than a polite and ego-salving *no*.

- *It seems slight* means in a picture book that it is not strong enough for 32 pages of illustration. In a novel it can mean characterization or plot are too weak to carry the length.

- *It has a certain amount of charm but . . .* usually means that while the writing is solid, the editor has seen too much of this particular kind of story.

- *Too quiet for us* usually has to do with the editor's evaluation of the marketplace; what the editor thinks will sell out there in the real world.

- *More a mass-market idea* is an educated judgment indicating the editor feels the book would do better with the kinds of publishers who produce the books that sell to super-market chains, books like *Strawberry Shortcake* and *Sesame Street*.

If the editor spells out just what he or she feels is wrong with the book but does not make an offer or ask to see the revised book, consider the criticisms carefully. Send a nice letter to the editor thanking him or her. And be sure to send that editor your next manuscript, citing the helpful rejection letter you received about your last submission, its title, and the date of the letter.

Of course, if the letter you receive is an acceptance letter, you have a whole new series of problems opening up before you. But they are problems that promise a happy ending.

There is, however, one kind of acceptance letter you must be wary of, and that is the one that says: "We want to publish your book, and it will cost you only $2,000." No reputable publishing company charges you *anything* for the privilege of publishing your book. *They* pay *you* for that privilege. A company that charges for the service is called a "vanity publisher." It is a glorified printing company that preys on the vanity of would-be authors. Never even send your manuscript to such publishers.

Write out of love, write out of instinct, write out of reason. But always for money.
—Louis Untermeyer

‖ 13

The Business Side

WONDER OF WONDERS, your book has been accepted for publication. With the number of books published, perhaps that should not come as a surprise, though I have always considered each sale a minor miracle. I celebrate each time with just as much joy as the first.

What can you expect—and what do you need to know—now that your book is to be published, especially if this is the first time for you? At this stage you may not yet have an agent (it is hard to get an agent in the children's field prior to having at least one published book to your credit), and will have to negotiate with the publishers on your own.

You will need to take off the *creative* artist hat and put on the hard-nosed *business* hat when considering the terms of your contract.

These terms will include how much money you will receive, how soon the book will be published, what happens if the book is sold to the movies or to a reprint house or to a foreign publisher. The contract will also spell out your responsibilities as author (no libel, no obscenities, no plagiarism, a clean copy of an acceptable manuscript), and the publisher's responsibilities (royalty statements at specified times, books kept in print as long as feasible).

If you have no idea what a good contract should contain to be fair to you and to protect your interests, keep in mind that reputable publishers do not take advantage of writers and they will undoubtedly give you their standard royalty contract. (You should not agree to a flat fee for the book in most cases.) After you have had some publication credits, you can become eligible for membership in such professional organizations as The Authors Guild (234 West 44th St., New York, NY 10036). Before publication, you can become a member of the Society of Children's Book Writers (see Chapter 11). Ask the organization for a good sample contract and specific advice on terms, usual advances against royalties, etc. A possible alternative is to consult a lawyer—though there are not many copyright or literary lawyers outside of New York or major cities. At the very least, have your editor explain the meaning of each of the clauses and subclauses to you.

Take special note of the "option" clause. This means the publisher gets a first look at your next book and must render a judgment by a specific time. If you keep that clause in your contract, be sure that the time specified is tied to when you submit that manuscript, not to the time your first book is published, for that may be years away. You can, of course, request that the clause be struck out, or modified to read "next book of a similar nature on terms to be agreed upon." The option clause is one of those good news/bad news items. It is good in that it indicates your publisher's desire and intent to publish more by you, and the willingness to promise a fast reading on subsequent manuscripts. It is bad in that it may bind you to a publisher even if they treat you shabbily. In my own contracts, option clauses are either severely limited or struck out altogether.

The words *advance* and *royalty* always seem to puzzle new authors, but there is nothing simpler. If you receive an advance against royalties of $1,000 and a 10% royalty, that means that when your book has sold enough copies so that your percentage of the take has made up that original advance, the publisher will start sending you more money at six-month intervals. It is a kind of loan (but be sure the contract says it is a non-returnable advance) and a kind of payment for your work already done. If your book sells for $10, with a 10% royalty you will receive 10% of every book sold, or $1 a copy. (Be sure the royalty advance is calculated on the gross or jacket price, not the net or received amount.) When 1,000 copies of the book have sold, you will have earned back $1,000—the advance. An advance is the publisher's way of telling you they expect the book to sell at least that much and are willing to give you that money up front. All other copies sold will be totaled by the publisher and your percentage sent on to you (or your agent, if you have one). It is important that you read your royalty statement carefully, checking the publisher's figures against the terms in your contract. Even with computers, errors can occur.

Time to revise

Once a book has been accepted and a contract drawn up, you (with many people in the publishing house) now have to turn your manuscript into a book.

The first job is usually the author's, for the editor may feel that the book still needs to be revised. I have always welcomed revising, though many people dread the return of the manuscript. Even the great Jonathan Swift wrote:

> Blot out, correct, insert, refine,
> Enlarge, diminish, interline;
> Be mindful, when invention fails,
> To scratch your head, and bite your nails.

But think of the word as *re-vision*. It means looking again, envisioning anew, seeing with someone else's eyes. It is a second chance at your dream. A second chance with the help of a professional, because the editor will have sent along a thorough revision letter or report. The manuscript may also be covered with what editors call *flags*, colored papers stuck onto your manuscript pages with questions, suggestions, and notes.

You might also be asked to come up with a new title. That may seem more difficult than it is. Usually you have appended a title at the beginning, and it has *become* the title for the sake of practicality. You are *used to* referring to your book by that title. The editor has looked anew at the book and may be able to see things more clearly. I originally called my Holocaust novel *Chaya* as I wrote, because it was the name of my main character. But when asked to come up with a better title, I looked again at the body of the text and came up with a number of suggestions, of which *The Devil's Arithmetic* seemed the best by far. My book *Greyling* was originally called *Silky*, but the editor thought that too soft and feminine a name for the main character, who was a boy. Titles are terribly important. They catch the reader's ear the way a book jacket catches his eye. A good title can be an aid in selling a book.

Editing

Once a book has been accepted, revised, titled, and returned to the publishing company, it is ready to be copyedited. That means someone at the publishing house will check your story word for word. The copy editor is looking for spelling errors, punctuation mistakes, misstatements of facts, etc. If you change the hero's eyes from gray to green halfway through the book, or fail to spell the heroine's name correctly, it is the copy editor's job to make it right. The copy editor is the last person to check the manuscript before it goes to the printer. There may be, and usually are, additional questions to be answered on your revised version.

The printer sets the book into galleys—long sheets of paper on which the complete text of your book is printed, in a typeface that has been selected by the publisher. Several sets of the galleys are sent back to the publishing company to be proofread and checked for errors, and one of these sets will be sent to you.

It will be the first time you will see your book in type. The feeling you have will be a combination of fright and flattery. Suddenly, the book is *real*. You sent out a typed manuscript, many of the changes inked in by you and the editors. And what you have seen sent back is Truth. It may be only a moment or it may be hours before you are ready to sit down and edit Truth, but edit it you must. With a good steady eye and a ruthless pen you must go over every last word, because this is probably the last time you will get to make any changes. After that, the book will be untouchable, set down in print with your name attached to it. But change or add or subtract at this point with infinite care. Changing what has been set into print is expensive, and by contract you may be charged for making too many changes.

If your book is a picture book or a book with pictures in it, the editor will have already talked to you about the illustrator to be chosen. If you are lucky (or if you insist) you will see sketches or a dummy or at least the final drawings before they are printed. Take time to look at them carefully with a copy of your text at hand.

Some artists don't read a manuscript with care, and add fillips in their illustrations that actually contradict the text.

If the text says that the cat has curly whiskers, for example, be sure the artist has not drawn straight ones. Presumably both the editor and the art director have already checked things out, but it is *your* name that will be on the book and so *you* must take great care as well. Remember, though, every artist is a creator and you must be tactful in pointing out where your creation and the artist's are at odds.

To understand the printing process, two helpful books are Howard Greenfeld's *Books: From Writer to Reader* and Uri Shulevitz's *Writing With Pictures*.

Author/editor—friend or . . .

You must not be afraid to ask your editor questions, or to mention any mistakes you find. First-time authors often fear that by making any kind of fuss, they will cause the editor to renege on publishing the book. But keep in mind it is more important to have the book published properly than published hastily.

The best kind of relationship an editor and an author can have is one based on mutual respect and an understanding of the problems both are facing. The writer and the editor, after all, need one another.

It is easy to see why the editor needs the author. Quite simply, there would be no book without someone creating it and putting the words down on the page.

But there are at least three good reasons a writer needs an editor: First, the editor has a broad knowledge of the field and, one hopes, a historical perspective of it. Second, the editor has an understanding of your book's marketability. (This is not an absolute knowledge, but, rather, "educated intuition.") And third—perhaps more immediately important to the author—the editor is a valuable second eye, reading and reporting accurately and constructively his or her reactions to the book.

It is far easier for an editor to find a good writer than for a writer to find a good editor. For this reason, when a writer has found a good editor, he or she will usually follow that editor from publishing house to publishing house.

What makes a good editor? I have six criteria:

1. *Honesty.* The editor must tell me at all times what is right and wrong with my writing. We must both be ruthless with my work, though a little tact would be preferable. I prefer revision letters to start with what is right about my story before I am told what is wrong!

2. *Responsiveness.* The editor must answer my phone calls and letters, because when I am miles away and unable to cope with problems, I'd like to know someone else believes in my talents. The editor must act not as if I were an annoyance, an intrusion into what I already know is a busy life, but rather a welcome interruption.

3. *Ombudsman.* The editor must be my personal representative to the publishing company, fighting the fights I might not even know I am having with production and sales department, school and library promotion people.

4. *Vision.* The editor must be able to see further than I can, beyond my words, to their meaning which may be obscure to me. The editor must help me pull those meanings from my words.

5. *Ego-tending.* The editor must be aware of me as a person, too, helping with the care and feeding of my ego when I need it. And be ready to kick me where it may do the most good, if I need that, too.

6. *Respect.* The editor must respect me as a writer; respect my vision, my talent, my integrity. In turn I will respect the editor's knowledge and competence and good eye and ear. And we both must respect the language—its beauty, its treachery, its power to change lives.

Becoming a book

After the galleys have gone back to the editor, the entire publishing company gears up. The printer makes the corrections and runs off page proofs. These are corrected and any last-minute changes that the editor feels must be made (checking with you for substantive ones) are done. Then the proofs go back to the printer, where the final complex machinery is set in motion. The presses roll out huge sheets of paper on which sixteen of your book's pages are printed at once on a single side of a big sheet of paper.

These proofs are once again read and checked by the publishers. If the book is a picture book, the color proofs are gone over in minute detail by the editor, the production staff, and the illustrator.

When the editor gives the final O.K., the printer makes any final corrections and adjustments, and then the presses roll! Enough large sheets are printed to make (for an ordinary children's book) between 10,000 and 15,000 copies—or the number of copies the publisher feels can be sold—which are then shipped to the bindery.

While the printer has been doing his work, the editor and designer have been busy with other details, such as choosing the binding for the book and the color and paper grade for end papers.

When the sheets arrive at the bindery, they are fitted onto another large machine that folds and cuts them on three sides and stitches them up the fourth. The pages are then bound, jackets (printed prior to or simultaneously with the book) put on, and first copies shipped to the editor, who fires one off with a congratulatory note to you.

And you have your book in your hands. Of course, this is a highly simplified version of the very complicated process that turns a manuscript into a book.

By contract, you will receive six to ten free copies of your book. You will no doubt show these off or give them to anyone who asks for a copy, until you remember that after those free copies are gone, you will have to *buy* any others. You will get a 40% discount, but you will have to pay nonetheless. Let your friends and relatives know early on that you would appreciate it if they *bought* your book!

Now you are a published writer! And the rest of the process is in the hands of the sales force, the promotion department, the reviewers, the schools and libraries, and—ultimately—the young readers. A process that once-upon-a-time took a single person with a goose quill pen making single copies of a handbound book is now big business. With the almost three thousand new children's books produced yearly, hundreds of people spend almost a year in the production of each—not counting *your* writing time.

And now the rewards

Is it worth it?

Yes. To begin with, the writing itself is worth it. If you do not enjoy the process of writing, of setting down your thoughts and ideas in an orderly fashion, then you should not be a writer. Some writers find it painful, though they are quick to admit that it is even more painful *not* to write. For my own part, I find writing the most invigorating, stimulating, exciting part of my life. I love to watch new stories appear, as if they are running off my fingertips onto the typewriter keys, printing themselves onto the paper while I watch.

It is worth it to work with a host of other creative people: the editor, art director, illustrator, publicity director. Their ideas can be stimulating; they can push you further than you ever dreamed you could go.

It is worth it the first time you look at your finished book. It may seem different from the book you had originally envisioned—after all, a number of other creative minds have been at work on it. But it is *your* book. *Your* name is on the jacket, on the spine, on the title page.

It is worth it when you are first reviewed. Whether that review is bad or good, *your* book has been noticed. One small warning: The state of reviewing children's books in this country has had a short and rather ignoble tradition. Except for *The Horn Book*, *The New York Times*, *Publishers Weekly*, *School Library Journal*, *Kirkus Syndicate*, and ALA *Booklist*, there are not a lot of regular reviews. Magazines and newspapers will sometimes review a few children's books at Christmas. But books do get reviewed in trade publications and library journals; your editor will probably send you copies.

It is worth it the first time you see your book in a library or bookstore, nestled among its peers.

It is worth it the first time you receive your royalty statement. Though only a few children's books become national best sellers—*Jonathan Livingston Seagull* by Richard Bach, *Watership Down* by Richard Adams, *The Light in the Attic* by Shel Silverstein, *Masquerade* by Kit Williams, *The Eyes of the Dragon* by Stephen King, and *The Polar Express* by Chris Van Allsburg—many others continue to sell from five to twenty years, and even longer. Most adult books, by contrast (even best sellers), tend to live and die each season like mayflies.

But it is most worth it when you receive letters from your

young readers: some are laboriously printed, some are on computer paper, some in that careful, round first script:

> Dear Ms. Yolen:
> I was going to write to Enid Blyton or Mark Twain but I hear they are dead so I am writing to you.

> Dear Ms. Yolen:
> Your books will live forever. I hope you live to ninety-nine or 100, but who cares.

> Dear Ms. Yolen:
> Would you please write to the publishers and tell them that they picked a wonderful book to publish?

And sometimes a letter arrives from an adult which so stuns you that you know being a writer was what you were meant to be:

> Dear Jane:
> I was working at a children's hospital as the person coordinating the child activity program. My main work with patients was with the children who were gravely ill, having chemotherapy, or in some other way needing real support. I often used play therapy techniques or puppets, but if children were too sick I would read to them.
> Ann Marie was an eleven-year-old girl who had been admitted by a doctor who didn't usually work with us. She had been sick for quite a while but not diagnosed, so by the time her therapy started she had many tumors. As the therapy started to kill the tumors, her kidneys and then cardiac system were also affected, so that she had to be transferred to ICU.
> It appeared that she had always been an isolated and protected child and the nurses referred to her as "young for her age."
> The day I was to see her I was apprehensive. The times I

had been in before she had been so sick and filled with IVs and tubes and monitors it was hard to think about the person inside that ailing repository of technology. I picked at random a couple of books from the shelf and went down to ICU.

At first all I could think of was how sick she was. Her eyes were half open and her skin was yellow. She hardly moved except to turn her eyes towards me when I came in. I was in gown and mask as were all three nurses in there. They were just finishing her peritoneal dialysis and preparing to leave.

I asked her what she would like me to read and she didn't answer. "Would you like me to choose?" She nodded. And then, Jane, when I started reading *The Girl Who Loved the Wind*, the whole scene changed. The humming and beeping machines receded, the fear and pain stepped back into the corners of the room. I read this child a story that was all about her life and leaving.

She was a child who had grown up behind protective walls. She too had felt the summons of the wind, "not always good, not always kind," and was deciding to leave her overly protected life.

When I finished reading the story we just sat for awhile in silence.

Two days later she was dead, her doctor and family shocked because it seemed so sudden, not expected.

I have always since then loved that story . . .

I know it truly served to comfort the departure of that child.

In the morning after her death, after we had cried and talked and wept about it, a beautiful stellar jay flew into our patio, came and sat on the arm of a chair and looked into the bedroom at me, still in bed. He sat there for almost a minute and I was filled then with a sense of peace. He seemed to say, "I come from Ann Marie and she's all right now."

These are things that you should know.

Is it worth it? If I had not written that book, one little

girl would have made a journey into the dark without the story-teller whispering into her ear.

Of course it was worth my effort and time and energy and love to write that book. For Ann Marie and for all the children, sick and well, who have been comforted and entertained and stretched and lent courage by my stories. And your stories. From our hearts to theirs; it is such a short and such a long lifeline.

Was it worth it? You tell me.

Index